WHAT THE CUSTOMER WANTS YOU TO KNOW

WHAT THE
CUSTOMER
WANTS YOU TO KNOW

How Everybody Needs to Think
Differently About Sales

RAM CHARAN

PORTFOLIO

PORTFOLIO
Published by the Penguin Group
Penguin Group (USA) Inc., 375 Hudson Street, New York, New York 10014, U.S.A.
Penguin Group (Canada), 90 Eglinton Avenue East, Suite 700, Toronto, Ontario,
Canada M4P 2Y3 (a division of Pearson Penguin Canada Inc.)
Penguin Books Ltd, 80 Strand, London WC2R 0RL, England
Penguin Ireland, 25 St. Stephen's Green, Dublin 2, Ireland
(a division of Penguin Books Ltd)
Penguin Books Australia Ltd, 250 Camberwell Road, Camberwell, Victoria 3124,
Australia (a division of Pearson Australia Group Pty Ltd)
Penguin Books India Pvt Ltd, 11 Community Centre, Panchsheel Park,
New Delhi–110 017, India
Penguin Group (NZ), 67 Apollo Drive, Rosedale, North Shore 0632, New Zealand
(a division of Pearson New Zealand Ltd)
Penguin Books (South Africa) (Pty) Ltd, 24 Sturdee Avenue, Rosebank,
Johannesburg 2196, South Africa

Penguin Books Ltd, Registered Offices: 80 Strand, London WC2R 0RL, England

First published in 2007 by Portfolio, a member of Penguin Group (USA) Inc.

1 3 5 7 9 10 8 6 4 2

Artwork and diagrams by the author

LIBRARY OF CONGRESS CATALOGING IN PUBLICATION DATA
Charan, Ram.
What the customer wants you to know : how everybody needs to think differently
about sales / Ram Charan.
p.   cm.
Includes index.
ISBN-13: 978-1-59184-165-4
1. Sales management.   2. Selling.   3. Customer relations.   I. Title.
HF5438.4.C43 2008
658.85—dc22   2007030980

Printed in the United States of America

To the hearts and souls of the joint family of twelve siblings
and cousins living under one roof for fifty years, whose
personal sacrifices made my formal education possible

Contents

WHAT THE CUSTOMER WANTS YOU TO KNOW

1

The Problem with Sales

The telephone rang. Charlie Baldwin knew he was about to get the news he had been waiting for since Monday. He had spent three months working on the sale, and if he got it he would make quota, get his bonus, and finally be able to take his wife Michelle on that trip to Europe he had promised her for years.

Charlie had no reason to doubt his good fortune. He was an experienced salesman for Sturgies Corporation, and had known Greg Lanterman, the customer's purchasing agent, for most of a decade. The two often spent long afternoons on the back nine, playing golf and sharing stories about their families. Both had two kids graduating from high school in the fall, and this only strengthened their bond.

When they had met last Thursday for drinks Greg did everything but promise Charlie the order—it was in the bag. That's why Charlie was stunned when he heard Greg's voice on the line. From his tone alone Charlie knew something was terribly wrong.

"Charlie, I did everything I could," explained Greg sheepishly, "and until about four days ago I was sure that my recommendation to give you the order was a shoo-in. But the CFO and the executive vice president of marketing intervened and decided that the sale should go to Progis Corporation. Your price was better, but the sales rep at Progis, Mark Logan, showed us how his approach would increase our cash flow and revenue growth. Mark also had some good ideas that our executive vice president of marketing said would help us to differentiate our brand. I'm really disappointed. In fact, I need to do a reality check on myself: I can't help but wonder if I'm losing credibility in the eyes of the higher-ups," Greg confessed.

Charlie's mind started to race. He knew Mark Logan. In fact, he had seen him more than once at the customer's office talking with people Charlie had never met. All of Charlie's contact was with Greg; he never gave Mark more than a passing thought.

"We had the cutting-edge technology, the lower price, and better cost savings for Greg's company," Charlie thought to himself. "I was sure we would win. But Mark Logan somehow beat me to the punch."

Charlie felt deeply disappointed, but for the first time, he also felt anxious. His wife Michelle had come into the room, and it seemed to her that the telephone call had aged him five years.

For the past 12 months Charlie has been on the receiving end of four similarly disappointing telephone calls. And these calls came from people he relied on the most—people like Greg, whom he had known and trusted the longest. Suddenly, fear struck him to his marrow. He doubted himself in a way that he hadn't for a very long time. "Have I lost my touch?" he wondered. He knew he had just lost his quota, his bonus, and would be forced to break his promise to Michelle about that long-overdue vacation. What he didn't know was whether or not he would still have his job this time next year.

Nobody bats a thousand. But when you keep losing sales despite having great products and services, it's time to take a step back. You have to reconsider what you're trying to accomplish and how you're going about doing it. In fact, it might be time to reinvent the way you sell.

Consider that the traditional sales process hasn't changed much for more than a hundred years. Its roots are in a time some five decades ago when supplies were tight and suppliers held the cards, when orders had to be booked weeks or even months in advance and customers, anxious for a steady supply of material and lacking information about availability, had little room to negotiate price. Salespeople were basically order takers. That situation might ring true today in some isolated cases—for critical parts or commodities like platinum—but those are the exceptions, not the rule.

As the number of suppliers has increased, salespeople have evolved from order takers to ambassadors, plying their social skills to learn what a customer needs and using their product knowledge to present products and services to match those needs. Salespeople built long-term relationships with purchasing agents, cementing those ties with golf games, skybox seats, and theater outings, and maybe taking the CEO to special events like the Olympics or the Super Bowl. Those relationships gave the salesperson an edge, provided he or she could meet the customer's requirements.

But now the context is completely different. In many businesses, there is a glut of suppliers and more suppliers entering the market everyday, and thanks to the Internet, they are easy to find. Every customer has access to prices and specifications from suppliers anywhere on earth. The asymmetry, or imbalance, of information has been corrected. At the same time, customers are under enormous pressure to deliver value to their clients and their shareholders. They are compelled to use the newfound power of transparency and overcapacity to drive down prices, resulting in an unprecedented degree of commoditization with sometimes devastating effects on sellers. Customers can play one supplier against the other in online auctions that force prices so low the seller can't make any money.

Under those conditions, long-standing relationships and good products are not enough. Sellers can have great strategies, differentiated technologies, faster product development cycle times, efficient operations, and good friends in the customer's shop and still not get the sale, or not at the premium prices they deserve. Margins are often squeezed, sellers can't retain customers, and top-line growth fails to materialize.

But the pressure on customers to perform is actually a huge opportunity for those suppliers who can help them. To be sure, customers must meet their financial expectations, but they also need to succeed in the marketplace. So while they want low prices, they also want their clients to love their products and services. They want to win against their competitors and stay ahead of them. They want to develop their business and improve their earnings, and they want to keep cash flowing in. In short, they want their business to succeed on many dimensions. And although they may not articulate it, they want suppliers who can help them accomplish those things by acting as partners, not one-time transactors.

Your customers want you to know how their business works, so you, the supplier, can help them make it work better. Here's the catch: you won't be able to do that with your traditional sales approach. The truth is that the long-neglected sales function is out of synch with current opportunities. Although management teams try to revive it with new sales incentive systems and new people, more radical change is needed.

This book is a guide to transforming the selling process to fit today's business world. It defines a totally new approach to selling that is both radical and practical. This new approach, which has been battle-tested in a number of companies and in a variety of industries, releases you from the hell of commoditization and low prices. It differentiates you from the competition, paving the way to better pricing, better margins, and higher revenue growth built on winning relationships with customers that deepen over time.

Turn Selling Around

The heart of the new approach to selling is an intense focus on the prosperity of your customers. This is a radical departure from what most salespeople and selling organizations do. The entire psychological orientation is shifted 180 degrees. No longer do you measure your own success first. Instead, you measure success by how well your customers are doing with your help. You're not focused on selling a specific product or service; you're focused on how your company can help the customer succeed in all the ways that are important to that customer. By tapping the many resources you have at your disposal to help customers meet their business goals and priorities, you are adding value.

This ability to create value for customers will differentiate you in a crowded marketplace, and you will be paid a fair price for it—one that is commensurate with the value customers perceive they are getting and the value you do in fact provide. I call this new approach *value creation selling,* or VCS.

Value creation selling is sweepingly different from how most companies sell today, in these ways:

First, you as a seller and your organization devote large amounts of time and energy—much more than you do today—to learning about your customers' businesses in great detail. What are your customers' goals? Which financial measures are they most keen about? How do they create market value and what are the key factors that differentiate their product or service from those of their competitors? Only then do you look for ways to help the customer in the short, medium, and long term. The greatest opportunities lie in the medium and long term, where you and your customer can work together to change the nature of the game in your customer's industry based on value you can help provide.

Second, you use capabilities and tools that you've never used before to understand how your customers do business and how you can help them improve that business. Sales is no longer just for the sales force: you need to muster the help of people in many parts of your company to do that. People from many different departments, including legal, finance, R&D, marketing, and manufacturing, become intimately familiar with your customer. You compile large amounts of information about your customer, both facts and impressions, in useful databases that are shared and used to determine the best approach for helping your customer win.

This will demand that you build new social networks, both within your organization and between your organization and the customer's shop. Information will have to flow in both directions, and there will be a need for frequent formal and informal interaction among people serving different functions within your company and between your company and the customer's. For example, your engineering people will need to meet with the people in your customer's shop who define the specifications of your customer's products or services.

Third, you're going to make it your business to know not only your customers but also your customers' customers. It is no longer enough simply to satisfy your customers' demands. You also have to know what motivates their customers. In order to tailor your solutions to your customers' markets, you have to know who their customers are, what they want, what their problems and attitudes are, and what decision-making processes they use. To devise unique offerings for your customer, your company must use its capabilities to work backward from the needs of the end consumer to the needs of your customer. This is the *customer value chain.*

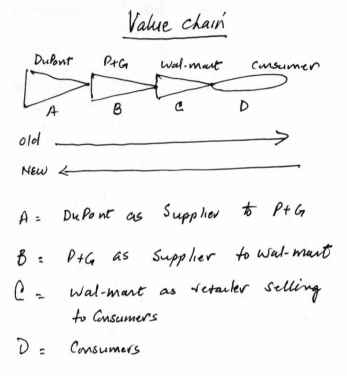

Value chain

A = DuPont as Supplier to P+G

B = P+G as Supplier to Wal-mart

C = Wal-mart as retailer selling to Consumers

D = Consumers

All Suppliers must learn Consumer insights.

Fourth, you have to recognize that the execution of this new approach will require much longer cycle times to produce an order and generate revenue. It requires patience, consistency, and a determination on your part to build a high degree of trust with your customers. This is imperative because in this new relationship the two-way information exchange is far deeper than what you have relied on in the past. But once it gets going, the cycle time can be very fast, because you will have established trust and credibility.

Finally, top management in your company will have to reengineer its recognition and reward system to make sure that the organization as a whole is fostering the behaviors that will make the new sales approach effective. Hitting quarterly sales targets is not the only basis for rewarding the sales force under this approach. Further, other members of the sales team from various functional areas must be recognized and rewarded proportionately for their contributions. If after receiving sufficient training and support the salespeople or other functional executives don't adopt the new approach with wholehearted enthusiasm, you will have to replace some people.

What the Sales Force Will Need to Know

Value creation selling entails profound changes in the sales force itself. Salespeople are no longer solo operators. Rather, they are team leaders, responsible for organizing and directing groups of experts from such diverse areas as finance, legal, and manufacturing in their own organization. Your company's support functions will need to work in earnest with the sales leaders, synchronizing their priorities with the needs the sales leader lays out. (See the illustrations comparing conventional selling with VCS.)

This is a role salespeople are unaccustomed to, and many will at first be uncertain about their leadership abilities. But most salespeople have good interpersonal skills. Many will excel in coordinating their colleagues' efforts and will enjoy doing it.

Conventional Selling

Vendor → get Sale. Get Price → Sales Person ← Get Discount ← Customer / Purchasing

- information is now less opaque

Value Creating Selling

VENDOR   CUSTOMER

L {M₁
M₂ } S₁   → Sales Team ←   F L M₁
T   P M₂ S₁
F₁   T
S₂ }   S₂

INFORMATION FLOW - both ways.

S_1 = Sales person; S_2 = Supply chain; M_1 = Mfg; M_2 = Mktg; T = Technology; F_1 = Finance; L = Legal; P = Purchasing

. Information will also flow from Vendor's people directly to Customer's people as the trust builds.

Salespeople will have to master a new body of knowledge and analytical tools in order to earn the respect and cooperation of their team members. They will need the ability to research and understand the customer's business, including the customer's market segments and trends in the customer's industry, and most important, how the customer's business makes money now and how it will continue to make money in the future. To gain that knowledge salespeople will frequently call upon their teammates to engage with people in the customer's shop. The teammates will develop their own connections inside the customer's company and contribute their insights to help the team develop a view about future trends and game-changing ideas to help the customer.

Probably most daunting to salespeople, they will have to become diagnosticians. Using their own knowledge and all the other capabilities necessary from within the selling organization, the salesperson must develop a very clear and specific definition of the customer's *business* needs. They must tap the creativity and expertise of their colleagues to shape some alternative offerings to satisfy those needs, and test those alternatives by engaging with people in the customer's organization, but the salesperson takes the lead. Finally, he or she must refine the value proposition and be prepared to demonstrate, especially to key decision makers, how the customer's business stands to benefit.

Value creation selling does not end once the sale is made. Interactions among the various people of the customer's organization and the selling organization must continue after the sale. That is a critical part of building the trusting relationship necessary to develop future value propositions, including some with longer time horizons. The salesperson must ensure not only that the solution actually produces the promised results, but also that the continuing dialogue with the customer is forward looking, energizing, and aimed at creating game-changing ideas.

If you think about the many ways in which the sales job changes, you'll realize that something important happens: the salesperson who can execute this approach is transformed into a potential general manager, with all the decision-making, analytical, leadership, and profit and loss (P & L) responsibilities that are part of that job. The company gains a source of general management talent that it didn't have before and salespeople have a new career track. The more successful among your salespeople can easily move into a variety of high-level jobs, particularly as heads of P & L centers or business units, or even eventually the CEO job.

The Promise of Growth

Value creation selling is about re-creating the front end of the company with a sense of urgency and appetite for change that reflect what's at stake. The successful execution of VCS will provide your company with significant benefits, both internally and in the competitive marketplace. If you are among the first in your industry to adopt it, you will have a significant competitive advantage. This book can help you get where you need to go. It provides the tools, the ideas, and the methodology you need to train and support people in the selling organization and execute the sweeping corporate changes that will be required. It provides guidance not just for salespeople and sales managers but also for the many people throughout your company who will be active participants in value creation selling. It is relevant for any business-to-business company, a term that encompasses nearly every company in one way or another. These companies must escape the commodity pricing that is part of simple transactional selling and become sources of value creation for their customers.

There is no quick fix. If there were, most people would have made it long ago. But those leaders who are forward looking, who have the temperament to implement value creation selling and stay with it, will enable their companies to win on a consistent basis. Suppliers that create real value for customers will stand out against the competition and get a better return on their great strategies, innovations, and talented people.

Let me give you some examples of how value creation selling can be used in different industries. Software is generally sold to a customer's chief information officer. The salespeople calling on the CIO generally base their pitch on the costs it will help the customer reduce. Think about this: What if they could show a bank how the software could help that bank retain a client or better tailor its products or services to its client? The salesperson would be demonstrating how her company's product creates value for the customer. Value creation selling in this context is about increasing revenue, not just reducing costs.

Communications companies like Cingular, Verizon, and Vodafone sell their offerings to large multinational companies such as IBM, American Express, General Electric, and Siemens. For the most part, those sales take place based on the price of the offering. If, instead, the vendors could show their customers that modifications to their communications networks can increase revenue or cash flow, they would have a much more powerful case to ask for and get a premium price rather than a discounted price. They would be creating value.

Many pharmaceutical companies market their drug products directly to third-party insurance companies like United Healthcare, WellPoint, and Aetna. As in so many other business-to-business transactions, the negotiations are about price. But as consumers and government regulatory agencies turn up the pressure to keep a lid on drug costs, the pharmaceutical companies' sales forces have a role to play in helping their large customers understand their constituencies. That can help create value.

In the consumer packaged goods arena there are huge producers like P&G, Colgate, and Unilever and equally large retailers like Wal-Mart, Target, and Walgreens. In the past the producers and the retailers battled one another over price. But today they are increasingly working hand in hand to find ways to bolster revenues, increase cash flow, and achieve higher turnover per square foot of shelf space. And while the retailers, especially Wal-Mart, have a fearsome reputation for extracting the last tenth of a cent from their suppliers, I have witnessed one producer increase its gross margin over a 20-year period from 40 to 60 percent while selling through Wal-Mart and Target. The tight-fisted retailers allowed those margins because the producer's managers and sales force demonstrated that their products would increase the retailers' revenue and inventory turns. They were creating value.

In Japan, Tyco Electronics supplies equipment to Toyota. But the relationship is far from arm's length. Instead, Tyco has its people in Toyota's factories, where they can ensure the performance of Tyco's products while looking for new ideas to improve Toyota's cars. In a three-year period Tyco may bring Toyota as many as twenty-five important new ideas that increase the attractiveness, efficiency, or reliability of Toyota automobiles around the globe. Tyco is in reality selling value, not just products, to Toyota.

Opportunities abound. But you might have to make some significant changes to your business if you want to pursue them.

2

Fixing the Broken Sales Process

Remember how depressed Charlie became when he got the bad news about losing the sale to Mark Logan's company? Unfortunately for him, that was not his last telephone call of the day. He had to call Susan Kipp, the executive vice president of sales, to report that the business they had been counting on had fallen through. And Susan had to make that same phone call to Jack Garrett, the company's CEO.

The next morning's executive meeting was one of sober reflection. The leadership team agreed that Charlie's call was not an exception: the sales force as a whole seemed to be performing worse than the competition. The company was not getting the number of orders and the pricing it deserved for its cutting-edge technology and top-shelf customer service. Yet no one could explain why that was.

To Jack, it was one of the gloomiest executive meetings he could remember. He and his management team knew, and Wall Street appreciated, that his firm was ahead in technology, had a superior strategy, and was cost-efficient. Yet all of those factors were not compelling enough to win new business and, more important, to get premium pricing for the company's offerings.

After the meeting, on his way back to his office, Jack reflected on the business. Technology was working well, operations were working well, and the strategy was sound. They had been putting a lot of pressure on sales and had changed the incentive system twice. Jack had tremendous confidence in his head of sales as well. What they hadn't done, however, was a thorough reevaluation of the selling process. It occurred to him that while they had streamlined and modernized other areas of the business in recent years, the selling process itself had remained untouched. Maybe it was time for some fresh thinking.

We have to face the truth: *the process of selling is broken.* Customers have more choices today and are under intense pressure to deliver results. Yet few companies change the way they sell in the face of this reality. When they don't, a lingering malaise sets in as sales continually underdelivers and senior leaders continually fail to get the top-line growth they need.

You know your sales process is out of date when these things are true:

Your sales force interacts mostly with your customer's purchasing department. I know, that's the way it's always been. But a purchasing department is merely the order executor for the decision makers in the customer's shop. Those decision makers are in functions such as sales and marketing, product design, engineering, and manufacturing. The fact is, you're isolated from your customer's most important people.

The entire discussion about a possible sale revolves around price. The salesperson does a great job of articulating what the product can do and extolling the virtues of the company's reputation and brand, but the basis of the discussion is price. Even then, the price that results from those negotiations doesn't often stick. The customer continues to press for volume discounts, freight charges,

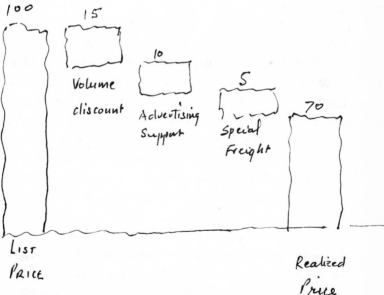

FINAL REALIZED PRICE

advertising support, tooling costs, and technical support—all of which come out of your pocket, in effect reducing the real price. This phenomenon is all too common. The illustration above shows how the price (and therefore profitability) of the sale gets eroded after the terms are supposedly set.

Sales training consists mostly of highly focused, exercise-based training that shows salespeople how to not take no for an answer, how to not knuckle under to pressure, and how to bring home the bacon without compromising on price. I admit that this kind of training, which often involves role playing and inspiring videos of the best closers, can buck up a sales staff's spirits, at least for a while. But because it isn't addressing the real problems between the supplier and the customer, it doesn't produce much in the way of improved results. The effects quickly fade.

Top management is constantly fiddling with the incentive schemes for the sales force to toughen them to get better pricing and better margins. The incentives for the sales force are commonly designed on a quarterly basis and linked to the booking of revenue and orders. Manipulating the incentive system puts pressure on salespeople to mentally explore myriad ways to close the deal without agreeing to price reductions. None of this, however, creates value to the customer. Instead, you are simply changing negotiating techniques and putting more stress on an already overstressed sales force. You create a situation in which the sales force does more, but of the wrong things.

The sales force that seems spread too thin is reorganized to bring a more intense focus on customers. This certainly allows each salesperson to spend more time with his or her customers, but to what end? Again, since this doesn't solve the fundamental problems afflicting the sales process, it results in more man-hours to achieve approximately the same return. As we will see, this is sometimes a *necessary* move, but it is seldom a *sufficient* move.

Salespeople are not included in the design of the company's offering. Presumably the salesperson is the single person in your company who knows most about what customers want or need. Granted, the salesperson may not see the big picture and may not be aware of other motives you have for designing the product the way you do, but by excluding the sales force from the design process you rob yourself of their insights into the customer, and you rob them of the insights they need to present your product competently to the customer. It's a lose-lose situation for your company.

Little thought and even less interaction is given to your customers' customers. Your customer is desperate to make his customer happy. Presumably you know that, but what steps have you taken to find out how your product fits into the overall package your customer offers to *his* customers, or to his customers' customers? Sales is a kind of chain reaction. Only if the ultimate user of a product is happy will those who had a hand in it stand to profit in the long run.

Your salespeople are internally focused. You may not think your company suffers from this very common problem, but all you have to do is sit down with a salesperson and ask her how much of each day's job is spent doing administrative tasks and paperwork. Every minute is a minute that can't be spent face-to-face with a customer.

Sales management is convinced it's doing a good job.

Your sales management team is doing everything you want and have asked them to do. They don't understand any better than you do what is wrong. But the whole DNA of the sales force is focused on chasing orders, booking the revenue, being accessible to the customers and doing the necessary followthrough on their post-sale requests. Neither the sales force nor sales management has the business acumen and skills to intelligently analyze how the customer makes money, what the customer's financial and other priorities are, and how they relate to the seller's organization and offerings.

What You're Leaving on the Table

Fixing the broken sales process requires knowing precisely what the customer values: why he will prefer you over rivals and why he will continue to rely on you and sustain a trusting organizational relationship with you.

Lou Eccleston, the former president of global sales, marketing, and services at Thomson Financial and now CEO of Pivot Inc., argues that "making a sale is not the objective, it's just a symptom of a successful communication. It's a symptom that indicates you understand the customer and are measuring your success by your customer's success. Your success is governed by how well you understand what you can do to create value for the customer. If you can't impact the customer's performance in a positive way, then you're going to be a commodity product and you're going to get commodity prices."

Remember Charlie. What he was selling was his interpersonal relationship, the brand name of his company, and more important, a technologically superior product at a lower price than his competitors'. This translated into a cost reduction in the customer's shop, which Charlie was only too quick to point out. He described the return on the customer's investment quantitatively, calculating it based on the purchase price and a potential reduction in the customer's costs.

But the customer was focused on something else: accelerating revenue growth and increasing cash flow to fuel that continued growth. Charlie's competitor, Progis, was attuned to those priorities and found a way to help the customer generate cash by sustainably reducing inventories. It explained to the customer exactly how its offering would help the customer achieve its top priorities. The Progis value proposition met the customer's business needs far better than the one Charlie's company offered. This difference may seem subtle, but it is at the heart of value creation selling.

Cost reduction is the metric most salespeople think of and use when making their pitches to the purchasing people. If that's as far as you go, you're leaving a lot of value on the table. Every business has a combination of metrics by which it measures whether or not it is creating value for shareholders. (I'll explain these in a later chapter.) Even people without financial training can learn to understand them.

To help the customer succeed, you should consider how you can help improve several of these metrics. Say, for example, a software company is pitching its product to a pharmacy chain, knowing it will reduce the pharmacy's labor costs by $300,000 per year. The cost of the software product is $600,000. The pitch is the return on investment, or ROI, of 50 percent ($300,000 savings per year divided by the $600,000 software cost). This is how most selling companies calculate the benefits, though some might evaluate the savings over a longer period in which the system will be effective.

The competitor has a software offering that also sells for $600,000. It will reduce the customer's operating cost by just $250,000 a year. But this offering does something more. It flags the accounts receivable that are overdue and prompts management to take action to collect these receivables. That alone results in an additional cash flow of $325,000. What's more, this software, accompanied by additional training of pharmacy managers offered by the software seller, brings up daily lists of customers who should be getting prescription refills and prompts the pharmacy staff to contact them. These refills increase revenues by $400,000 a year, a benefit that adds an estimated $200,000 per year net profit to the bottom line. Thus if the competitor's offering actually works, its value proposition would include the following benefits:

- The customer's profits increase by $450,000 a year ($250,000 in operating cost reduction and $200,000 profit from the additional $400,000). Thus the return on investment is $450,000 divided by $600,000, or 75 percent.
- In addition, the customer's first-year cash flow increases by $325,000 because of improvement in account receivables.

There are very few companies that won't value accelerated profitable revenue growth more than they do cost reduction. By understanding and addressing the customer's needs beyond cost reduction, the second software company created a more compelling offer.

Getting from Here to There

By now you probably realize that value creation selling requires a different mind-set, new capabilities, and new ways of working. No doubt you're wondering if you and your company can make the change. The short answer, based on my observation of companies that have done it, is yes. Companies that have invested the time and effort to adopt this approach can attest that it works. Maybe the following story will convince you.

A few years ago I worked with Unifi Inc., a textile maker in Greensboro, North Carolina, that was in serious trouble because of a sudden surge of competition from China and India. The thirty-five-year-old manufacturer of petroleum-based textile products was suffering in head-to-head competition from low-cost producers that had burst onto the scene just six years earlier. Not only was Unifi losing business, but its customers, which turn Unifi's basic textiles into finished products like pants and shirts, were dying. Everything was about price, and it seemed there was simply no way a U.S.-based textile company could compete long-term on price against China and India.

"We were in a deep dark hole," recalls Brian R. Parke, chairman and CEO of Unifi. "We were beginning to think there wasn't a damn thing we could do to get out of it. Those were tough times psychologically—we were contemplating a future with nothing but grim news that would ruin people's lives."

In a last-ditch effort to save the company, Parke reduced his dilemma to two simple questions: "How well do we really know our customers?" and "Are we getting the price we deserve from them?"

As he pondered those questions, Parke began to rethink what and how they were selling. Knowing that Unifi's fate was intertwined with its customers', he began to wonder whether they were doing enough to help the struggling clothing manufacturers. Maybe they had to get more deeply involved in their customers' businesses as a way to save their own. He ultimately concluded that they needed to redesign their whole approach to selling and completely reorganize Unifi to carry it out. They had to be sure they were focused on the right customers and then go further to help those customers succeed. They would start by pulling together everything they knew about them.

Parke put Ben Holder, Unifi's chief information officer, in charge of creating a process to capture comprehensive information about each customer and building a network to share it. This effort was called the *profit growth initiative* (PGI). A CIO in charge of such an important marketing and sales initiative? That's just one example of Unifi's willingness to depart from business as usual. Parke knew Holder was the right person to systematize information that had to be collected and shared companywide.

The best source of that information, Parke and Holder realized, was the sales team. So for two hours every morning, five days a week, they met with the sales force, to find out what the salespeople knew about Unifi's business, their customers' businesses, and their customers' customers' businesses. As a first step, the senior leaders asked the salespeople to develop a detailed profile of a few of their favorite customers, which was to include their financial position and competitive strength, as well as their product needs. Each salesperson had to stand in front of the group and make a presentation about a particular customer and answer questions from his or her colleagues and the executives.

"We asked them all sorts of questions like, 'Who's the decision maker at the customer's shop?' We didn't mean to embarrass them, but to let them know that we needed those answers. They didn't think they could get the information about their customers' financial position, for instance, but we encouraged them to simply ask. Sometimes it worked, sometimes it didn't. And it took time, sometimes as long as ten weeks, to develop a decent profile."

These meetings were exceptionally unnerving for the salespeople, especially at the start. "The process was very upsetting to them," Parke explains. "They had been doing a good job, the way we had asked them to for thirty-five years. Then we come in and say we're changing the game. It created a huge fear factor. But we told them, 'Look, we feel just as bad as you do that we didn't learn to do these things before. We're in this together.'"

The second step was to use that profile to find a way to sell the customer 10 percent more than in the past. "We didn't ask our sales team to double the business. We wanted to try to turn the process into a success, so we went for singles and doubles instead of going for a home run every time. Once people saw that they could do it, we'd won their hearts and minds. We were pushing to begin with, but then all of sudden they got the bit between their teeth and we started seeing results."

The third step was an ambitious leap to have the salespeople develop account plans that laid out a meaningful goal and the strategy to achieve it. Each salesperson identified specific tasks that other people within Unifi would have to do to help meet that goal and attached a name and a deadline to each task. They had to identify possible reasons that they couldn't meet their ambitious new targets. The results, Parke told me, were frightening.

"What we found scared the life out of me," he says. "We had no idea how much bull we routinely put the salespeople through. Credit approval was slow, we couldn't get a sample into the customer's hands—the number of bottlenecks and blockages was just astounding. People were busy with all sorts of things. It wasn't a question of not working hard, but were we working on the right things? Were our efforts aligned with getting an order?

"We brought in the managers in charge of the areas where we had concerns and told them what a huge impediment they were to our progress. Nobody was spared. Over time, it worked. The support functions became more responsive. That gave the salespeople the confidence to push for an order because they knew everybody in the company was backing them."

The final phase was the most ambitious yet. In essence it got each salesperson into the mind-set of a chief executive officer, responsible for developing a business plan and executing it by using large amounts of hard data and tapping the skills of everyone in the company.

"We were asking them to tell us all about the dynamics of their market, do an analysis of their customers and their competitors, and then give us a business plan to build the profits," says Holder. "If they could show us a credible plan, we'd bring the resources to bear to make it happen. But it had to be fact-based and it had to stand up to scrutiny. It had to be a sound business plan, not just a bunch of unsubstantiated assumptions."

Not everyone in the sales force was willing to change. Some salespeople left the company and others were reassigned within Unifi. "One person who left was obviously a passive resister," Parke says. "He couldn't buy into the fact that he was being nailed down by data. Some salespeople like to dance and shuffle and they always have a thousand excuses. But the way we're doing it now, you're right out there in the open. You can't hide."

Admittedly, the change process took longer than anyone had expected. "We started too fast," Holder says. "We had to tell ourselves frequently to ease up. The word is *patience.* It takes an enormous amount of patience to make this selling approach work. On a day-to-day basis it was hard to see much progress, but when we stepped back every so often and looked at how we were doing, we could see some headway."

But today, the result of Unifi's profit growth initiative surprises even Parke and Holder. "Now we have a secret weapon," Parke boasts. "We've reorganized the entire sales force, increasing its profile within the company. The focus on customers is incredibly high. We have information on customers that is accessible to everybody in the company and we can watch trends as they develop. And our salespeople have become terrific business people,

developing the characteristics of CEOs. They understand
the financials, they understand the business, and they are
highly competitive. They can deal with customers one-
on-one at every level. Most importantly, they're always
asking what we can do to make the customer successful.

"Now we are seeing our customers get revitalized, and
our own prospects are completely reversed. It has been an
epiphany. We now believe passionately that it is possible
to get a higher price for your product by better understanding the market, the dynamics of the market, the
customer's business, and the customer's customer's
business."

Unifi broke free of toe-to-toe price competition with
low-cost producers by learning more about its customers'
businesses and helping them compete. Salespeople became
business thinkers, developing their business acumen to diagnose their own and their customers' businesses. They
shared information openly with others at Unifi, and senior leaders ensured that every function and department
supported the sales effort. Parke and Holder helped the
sales organization make the transition by drilling them in
small doses over time, discovering the blockages and resistance points, coaxing them to go back to the customer
when information was missing, and helping them round
out their picture of the customer's total business. That
kind of business thinking has now become a habit for the
sales force.

Parke and Holder also realized that sales alone couldn't
do the job; it took many people in the organization to deliver value to customers. They engaged face-to-face with
leaders at many levels who could have stymied their progress. They made it crystal clear that selling is a team sport

and everyone is a player. This meant that the entire staff, from the lowest levels to the top, had to change some aspect of their work. Also important, once they embarked on the path, they never looked back.

Value creation selling is within your reach if you are willing to make changes. The following chapters will show you how.

3

How to Become
Your Customer's Trusted Partner

The night following the depressing executive meeting, CEO Jack Garrett was having drinks with Philip Hayward, Sturgis Corporation's newest director. Not yet familiar with either the company or the industry, Phil had a lot to learn about the business and was prepared to pepper Jack with a whole host of questions as he tried to understand how Sturgis operates. One of his first questions was about revenue growth. Phil wanted to know why the company's top line wasn't improving.

"I confess I don't understand it, either," Jack said. "We've got a good strategy, our technology is world-class, and we've got a measurable cost advantage over the competition.

"But if things keep going like they are now," Jack continued, "this will be the third year in a row that we'll have lost market share."

"What's the competition doing differently to win share away from Sturgis?" Phil asked. "And what are we doing to counter that, besides trying to keep prices down?"

Those two simple questions galvanized Jack to suddenly reframe his thinking. "When I think about our own vendors, all they do is keep trying to beat each other on price," he told Phil. "They tell us how much money we can save if we go with them. But my biggest challenge is building revenues and stemming the erosion in market share. I can't recall any big supplier coming to us with ideas for generating more sales or winning more market share, the things we really value." Jack paused a moment, then continued in rising excitement. "If that's the kind of supplier we want to work with, then that's the kind of supplier we need to be. We have lots of talented people and great technology, but maybe we're not delivering what our customers really need.

"If that's the case, then we're going to have to learn a lot more about them—their goals and priorities, their competitive challenges. We can do that, but we'll have to create a dialogue with them and earn their trust. I wouldn't expect our salespeople to do this on their own. Other people at Sturgis will have to help them out, which means we'll have to change how we operate. This could be just what we've been looking for."

Phil was startled that his simple inquiry had touched off such a cascade of new ideas from Jack. It all sounded good, but this was just a conversation over drinks. Did Jack really mean what he was saying about changing the whole way Sturgis approached its customers? "We'll see," Phil thought to himself as he and Jack said good night.

As he drove home, Jack's mind was bubbling with all the things that would have to change—roles, responsibilities, rewards, relationships. He was undaunted, because he knew in his gut that it would reinvigorate the company.

The plan he was conceiving would have salespeople take the lead in gathering information about what was really important to a customer's business. They would enlist the help of their colleagues at Sturgis to brainstorm ideas to create value for the customer.

For this to take root Jack would have to win the strong commitment of the senior team. A meeting at headquarters wouldn't give him the time to fully explain. Too many interruptions, too many people sneaking peeks at their BlackBerrys or slipping out to make a phone call. It had to be a two-day off-site meeting at which he and his team could thrash out the issues.

Jack's off-site was a success. By the end of it, the team had agreed on a new mission: become our customers' trusted partner. They defined the initiatives that would bring those words to life, and Jack made a personal commitment to follow through on them. With that, Sturgis began to reinvent its selling process.

Value creation selling is a customer-centric strategy. That means the customer is at the center of everything a company does. Alas, that isn't often the case. Before Thomson Financial began to implement a VCS strategy, Lou Eccleston tried a little experiment.

"I went around and I asked everybody I saw what were their great achievements in the last year. And not one person's answer included the word 'customer,'" he says. "There was stuff about 'I integrated twelve products into one' or 'we migrated this to that' or 'we had four product launches' and 'we hit this target or that target.' But not one person mentioned the customer. Now I know we're progressing because people are not only talking about the customer, their actions are about the customer. We've got more to do, but clearly we've made immense progress."

Information: The Heart of VCS

Information—lots of detailed information, both facts and impressions—is at the heart of value creation selling. The concept is simple: The more you know about your customer, the better you and your company will be at identifying his concerns and devising products and services that will help address them.

In the broadest sense you want to learn about your customer's opportunities and the competitive dynamics confronting his company. The key here is to analyze the customer's market growth and positioning.

As a salesperson you may think you already know a lot about your customers. But once you start an in-depth search for information about a customer you'll be amazed at how much more you can learn. Consider, for example, your customer's organizational structure. It's easy enough for an outsider to draw up an organizational diagram for most companies that shows the top management: the

CEO, the president and chief operating officer, the chief financial officer, the executive vice president of sales and marketing, the chief information officer, the vice president of manufacturing, and so on. If you know a little bit about the company you can even fill in the direct reports for many of those senior people. And there are some departments—purchasing, for instance—in which you drill down pretty deeply to identify specific people who report to the executive in charge of purchasing. But if I asked you who in that organization actually makes the decisions about the kinds of things you have to sell, could you answer that question with a high degree of certainty?

While you may think the purchasing department is making the decision, your friend the purchasing agent knows a lot more than you do about the situation. He may know, for example, that his company is having financial difficulties and it's the chief financial officer who is making the calls on what to buy, how much, and at what price. Or your friend in purchasing may know that his company is trying to win a new account and the executive vice president of sales and marketing has overridden the purchasing department's recommendation and ordered instead from a supplier whose price is a little higher, but whose product, when incorporated into your customer's offering, is more likely to impress or appeal to the account that your customer wants to land. Thus we can see that it isn't just the *quantity* of information that you have about a company, it's also the *quality* of that information. Knowing your customer's organizational chart is part of the quantity. Knowing who really makes decisions is quality information. Quality information makes all the difference in how well you understand your customer and are able to develop and sell value propositions that address the customer's opportunities and challenges.

So how do you get that kind of information from your customer? Much depends on the nature of the relationship. Turn the tables for just a moment and think of yourself as a customer. Let's say an insurance agent is calling on you to pitch a health insurance policy to your company. You've never met the guy before and don't know much about his company. When he starts asking you about the average age of your workforce, what kind of claims history your company has had over the past five years, and how many times OSHA has cited your factories for safety violations, what's your likely reaction?

Exactly. It's none of his business. That isn't true, of course. In his business he needs that information to calculate what premium his company will charge for a policy covering your company. But you don't know anything about him, and consequently you don't trust him. Therefore you're on guard and wary about sharing any of that sensitive information with him.

A few days later the representative of the company that currently provides health insurance to your firm stops by for a visit, and the situation is very different.

"How are things going?" he asks.

"Well," you respond, "several of our employees have complained to the benefits department about how little you're reimbursing them for outpatient surgery. They say you're not paying nearly enough for the facilities use at the outpatient center, just for the surgeon and anesthesiologist."

"Tell your benefits guy to send me those patient files and I'll look into it," he says. "We'll work with our outpatient surgical centers to get this issue resolved."

Here's a long-time rep for a supplier of services who you know well and trust. You're willing to share a lot more information with him both because you trust him and because he promises that he can solve a problem you're having. That's the kind of relationship you want to have with your customers. To achieve that, you've got to work hard to be worthy of your customer's trust.

The simple truth is that trust is built over time. Hopefully your relationship with your customer's purchasing department is on a sound footing. The customer knows you'll deliver on time, that your product meets the specs, and that you'll follow up on any after-the-sale problems. If you don't have that kind of reputation with the customer, you've got some serious remedial work to do before you can begin to think about adopting value creation selling. And of course, sometimes there won't be anything you can do: some customers won't want to share information with anyone else under any circumstances. You've got to focus on customers who are at least open to the idea.

Once you've established a basic reputation for trustworthiness with the customer, it's time to start gathering more information. The kind of information you want varies and will come from different sources. But the best place to start is with the information that your customer wants you to know. Just understand from the outset that this is the kind of information customers want you to know *only if they trust you.*

The better you understand and meet your customers'

needs, the more trusted you become. Over time, the barriers between your company and theirs drop and you become a partner they turn to for help. Your success is a natural product of the success you help them achieve.

To become a customer's trusted partner, you must understand the following:

1. The customer's set of opportunities and the anatomy of the competitive dynamics
2. The customer's customers and the customer's competitors
3. How decisions are made in the customer's organization
4. The customer's company culture, its dominant psychology and values
5. The customer's goals and priorities, both short-term and long-term, clearly and specifically

Let's take a little time to examine in more depth what they mean both for you and your customer.

The Customer's Set of Opportunities and the Anatomy of the Competitive Dynamics

Knowing a customer's competitive environment and potential opportunities is a good starting place to identify combinations of products and services that could help the customer compete better. Does the customer aim for technological superiority as, for example, Intel does with its proprietary manufacturing processes? Or is it trying to win by being the low-cost producer and expanding the market, as Dell did with its unique combination of a hyperefficient supply chain and build-to-order sales system? Or take Target and Wal-Mart. Both sell at prices well below those found in major department stores. But Target sells to a clientele with relatively higher incomes, offering them more fashion and aesthetics and a more enjoyable shopping experience. Wal-Mart seeks suppliers who can constantly wring costs out of their products. Target focuses on value creation, actively seeking special designers and manufacturers to produce the products it sells, often exclusively.

Other companies are expert at creating new market segments, tailoring products to appeal to different buyers through such features as design, functionality, or pricing. They can often mine supposedly mature markets by finding niches or subsegments for growth. They invest their energies in discovering insights into consumer behavior and figure out what offerings work and which ones don't. Importantly, they look to their vendors for innovative ideas that could help create and build a new segment before their competitors catch on. For example, Toyota, with its Lexus line, created a market segment between Mercedes-Benz and Cadillac where there was none before. That segment has since experienced tremendous growth. Any supplier working with Toyota and using value creation selling techniques to come up with innovative ideas that help Toyota get bigger margins or higher revenues will prosper as Toyota prospers. And Lexus wasn't Toyota's only triumph. More recently it virtually created the market for hybrid vehicles and is the dominant player in that category, yet another opportunity for creative suppliers to provide ideas to help Toyota continue to prosper.

No picture of a customer is complete without an understanding of the competitive intensity that the customer faces. There are many consumer businesses in which a David is up against a Goliath. Yet Davids are constantly winning, because they come up with irresistible offerings—think Apple. If you've got a David among your customers, can you bring an innovative idea that makes the customer's offering so distinctive that it can outgun the power of heavy advertising? That is an example of value creation selling that works backward from the consumer to the customer's customers and finally to the customer itself.

The Customer's Customers and the Customer's Competitors

The next most important thing to understand about your customer is her customers. Most companies have a minimum of one, two, or even three intermediaries before the seller's product, in some form, reaches the final consumer. For example, DuPont supplies its ingredients to Procter and Gamble, P&G makes an offering to Wal-Mart, and Wal-Mart reaches the consumer. Thus we have the customer value chain introduced in Chapter 1. With such companies, value selling gets a bit more complicated.

Who is your customer trying to sell his product or service to, and what are the criteria those buyers are setting? The answer can be complicated. Assume for a moment that your company manufactures a component that your customer uses as part of the consumer product he makes. Your customer's first-line customer, the one who buys it directly from your customer, may be a retailer, perhaps a chain of hardware stores in the southeastern United States. But as important as that retailer is to your customer's sales, the consumer who walks into that hardware store and makes a choice about which among competing products to buy is equally important. If the consumer won't buy your customer's product off the retailer's shelf, then it won't be long before the retailer quits buying it from your customer. Whether or not your customer is doing the kind of research that identifies such problems, you still need to do your own. Not only will you bring a different perspective to the analysis of buyer behavior; you'll also understand in detail what role your product plays in the sale of your customer's product both to the retailer and the consumer.

You can't really understand who your customer's customers are without also understanding who your customer's competitors are. By definition, competitors are all trying to appeal to the same customers. Believe me, your customer spends a lot of time worrying about competitors. Are they coming out with a new product with new features? Are they cutting the price simply to get rid of excess inventory or have they changed their product to make it cheaper to manufacture? How much are they spending on marketing and advertising? Why did that one competitor fire the vice president of product development? You need to know which competitors your customer regards as the biggest threat and why. If Alpha Company is the biggest threat, is it because it innovates faster or because it has newer and more efficient factories? Maybe it's simply that Alpha has the financial clout to spend more on advertising.

How Decisions Are Made in the Customer's Organization

I've already talked about how a company's organizational chart is a superficial rendering of the actual organizational structure. It's a place to start, but you'll need to know a lot more about how the company *really* works. As you probe and ask questions and learn more about your customer, you'll find some surprises. There will be people with powerful titles, for example, who really don't have much power. There will be other people who don't have impressive titles but exercise a lot of power. There will be subtle alliances between departments or divisions within your customer's shop that won't be apparent at first, and there will be equally subtle hostility between others. There will be some up-and-coming young executives who are destined to rise high in the organization (or to be recruited away if they don't get promoted fast enough), and there will be some placeholders, older executives who have burned out or lost their ability to change with changing circumstances, but who manage to hold on to their jobs. Some executives will be good delegators. Knowing who reports directly to them will be almost as good as knowing the executives themselves. Other senior managers will be classic micromanagers who want to stick their fingers in every pie.

What you really want to know is how decisions are made and who makes them. The key here is to follow the money. Work backward after identifying whose budget in the customer's shop will foot the bill for your offerings. Second, identify all players who will be involved in the purchase decisions. Some will be lower-level people whom you have never met or spoken to but who nonetheless have a voice in the decision. You want to know what sources of information these people use as the basis for their decision making. Can you work with these people to find possible new sources of information that might influence their decisions? It can help to review previous decisions to see if you can figure out the path that information takes through the decision-making process. What financial factors seem to be driving the decision making? As you're absorbing all this information be sure that you identify the up-and-comers in the customer's shop. They're your future contacts as you expand and deepen your relationship with the customer.

I call the sum total of how the people in a company work together (or don't) the company's social system. Understanding the social system in the customer's shop—who makes decisions, who shares information, who exerts influence, who throws up roadblocks—is an important piece of the puzzle when it comes to learning about problems and opportunities and crafting value propositions to address them.

The Customer's Corporate Culture, Its Dominant Psychology and Values

Every company has a unique culture, and you should understand what it is in your customer's shop. The symptoms of a corporate culture are always apparent. In some companies, for example, the culture revolves around hard-edged negotiations in which the customer's people feel compelled to win big concessions. Wal-Mart is probably one of the best examples of that kind of culture, often fighting to wring out the last tenth of a cent from the cost of something it purchases. But there are other companies that willingly pay for good aesthetics and design and believe that the best vendors should prosper alongside them. Target, Wal-Mart's arch rival, is a good example of this kind of culture. Cultural values typically include some level of integrity. It is sufficient to reach a mere verbal agreement with some companies. Their word is their bond and the contract is a mere formality. Other companies may sound like they've agreed to a set of terms, only to show up at the contract signing with myriad revisions, objections, and side provisions.

The Customer's Goals and Priorities, Both Short-Term and Long-Term, Clearly and Specifically

Chances are that if you asked your salespeople today whether they understand what their customers really care about, they would assure you that they do. After all, most have been exposed to PowerPoint presentations in which the customer lays out the company's vision, mission, values, and strategies, and most have got the message that price matters. But salespeople rarely have a full picture of where the customer's business is headed, what targets they are trying to reach, and how they plan to reach them. It takes business acumen to figure that out.

By business acumen, I mean the ability to understand the fundamentals of the business: profit margin, cash generation, return on investment, velocity, and growth. If you understand these things even at their most basic level, you will have insight into how the customer's business makes money and what goals and priorities they are pursuing, or perhaps should pursue. As you shape value propositions around those goals and priorities, you will be speaking the customer's language.

Almost all corporations have quantified goals, both for the short term and the long run, and ideas about what they will do to reach them. Often these goals and priorities can be discerned from company proxy statements, security analyst reports, and investor conference calls and communications to employees via the Web, e-mail, or a broadcast on the company's intranet. You'll need to understand which goals are most important at any given time, and why. Businesses are always making trade-offs. If cash flow is currently most important for a company, for instance, it may have to forgo some revenue growth for the time being by dropping some products or market segments.

Acquiring this knowledge may sound like a daunting challenge. It isn't, as I will explain shortly. And it is well worth the effort. A sales force that understands the financial fundamentals and trade-offs has an enormous advantage in becoming a trusted, long-term partner. For example, Motorola is engaged in a fierce battle for cell phone market share with Nokia, which has the world's largest share. Among Motorola's many component suppliers for its handsets is a relatively small North Carolina company called RFMD. Motorola's RAZR, their famous handset known for its strikingly slim design, gave Motorola a leg up in that competition a few years ago. But, as usual in this cutthroat business, Nokia and other competitors came back fast and hard, and in the fall of 2006 RAZR's market share began to decline; this resulted in lower profits and declining cash flow. Motorola had to make a decision: chase market share with lower price or find ways to fight back and restore the brand equity and profitability of the handset division.

Motorola decided to avoid the low-price, low-margin battleground and fight instead to maintain leadership in styling and functionality. That's all the people at RFMD needed to know. From engineers to designers to salespeople, RFMD is now focused entirely on providing Motorola with the components that will give it both a technology and style edge over other competitors, and providing them fast. RFMD is Motorola's partner in the big company's bid to hold the high ground in an incredibly competitive market.

Developing Your Business Acumen

In value creation selling, business acumen is a necessity. It is the basis for creating value propositions that speak to a broader and more meaningful set of customer's needs.

Even if you have never thought much about it before, you must now.

Business acumen is not an arcane or complicated skill. Every successful businessperson has business acumen, including unschooled vendors who sell their wares in third-world open-air markets. I grew up in a small village in India and learned the basics of business at a very early age while working in my family's shoe shop. If you think about those business fundamentals in their simplest terms, the way a street vendor selling fruits and vegetables in my native India might think about them, I believe the concepts are easy enough for anyone interested in business to understand.

Let's start with *profit margin,* something you probably already know a lot about. Revenue is the amount of money that comes into a company from the sale of its products or services. For a street vendor, it's the money he collects for selling his fruit and vegetables. Profit is the money left after deducting the cost of those goods. Profit margin is often stated as a percentage—how much money you get to keep as a percentage of the total revenues. If our vendor sells $150 (6,000 rupees') worth of fruits and vegetables, and they cost him $135 to buy, his profit is $15. His profit margin is 10 percent, or $15 profit divided by $150 in total sales.

The street vendor makes many decisions during the day to achieve his profit margin goal, beginning early in the morning when he decides how much fruit to buy and what to pay for it. Should he buy one variety or several? This will be his "product mix." As he sets up his cart, he decides how to price the fruit, which will affect his margin. During the day, he makes some tough trade-offs about what price cuts he should make to unload his inventory so he ends the day with enough cash to buy merchandise tomorrow. He learns how to make these trade-offs through trial and error. The clearer his view of his customers, the better his decision making will be. It's no different for big companies. General Motors, for example, has to decide what vehicle models to produce, how many of each to manufacture, and whether to offer sales incentives when inventory piles up on dealers' lots. It has to know consumers well to make decisions that have a favorable effect on margin.

Just as street vendors need *cash,* so do companies. A dwindling flow of cash from operations can get them in trouble, even if the financial statements show a handsome profit. Timing matters. Sometimes cash generation and cash availability are more important to a customer than profit. Such is the case for legacy airlines in the United States.

The next fundamental that concerns your customers is *velocity,* what some people call asset turns. Most companies' assets include equipment, buildings, and computer systems, plus accounts receivable and inventories. Velocity is how much annual revenue the company generates for each dollar it has invested in assets. If a company has annual sales of $1 billion and its total assets are worth $100 million, its velocity is 10. A retailer with $700 million in revenue and $100 million invested in inventory will have a velocity of 7. Velocity of 7 is quite good in retailing.

Vendors that deliver a value proposition to help customers increase their annual revenues for the same amount of inventories—for example, by replenishing store shelves more frequently and providing more appealing displays—increase their customers' velocity. This is highly attractive to customers because they can generate more sales with the same amount of cash, and their margins might also increase. That is an appealing proposition.

While margin and velocity are important in and of themselves, they combine into one measure most investors use to assess a business, and that is *return on investment.* Return on investment is simply margin multiplied by velocity ($R = M \times V$). Retailing is a low margin, high velocity business. A retailer might have 3 percent margin and velocity of 7, for a respectable 21 percent return. At the other end of the spectrum are telecommunications carriers. Their margin is about 12 percent. But they have a lot of investment in the ground, so their velocity is low, say around 1.5. Their return is 18. Both types of business attract investors. Each requires different ways to improve the business fundamentals.

Every company is also concerned about *growth,* at least to some degree. Most companies want growth that is profitable; they don't want to sacrifice margins for the sake of more revenue. That isn't always easy to achieve. One of your major challenges with at least some of your customers will be to help them achieve both revenue growth and profit growth.

Whether you're a street vendor or a corporate giant, *customers* matter. A growing market share shows that customers are choosing your product over your competitors' products in increasing numbers. In the early days of cell phones, few people owned one. That market has since gone through the roof, with hundreds of millions of cell phones sold each year. Having a growing share as the overall market is growing is a great position to be in.

Compact discs had their heyday when they replaced vinyl records and cassette tapes, but now new music recording and distribution technologies are cutting into CD sales. Soon the number of music CDs sold each year will begin to decline precipitously. Having a large market share of an industry in decline isn't so great. Knowing the size of your customer's markets, whether they are growing or shrinking and what its share of those markets is, will help you diagnose and solve problems.

Customer satisfaction is a big part of the market share equation. A happy customer tells others about the product and returns to buy more. When Japanese cars like Toyota were first imported to the United States in the 1960s they weren't particularly attractive to many American car buyers because they were small, comparatively underpowered, and not very well built. But as we know, the Japanese studied the American market carefully, fixed the perceived problems, and were soon offering higher-quality products at lower prices than Detroit. Today Toyota and Honda consistently rank highest among the world's automakers for consumer satisfaction, particularly in measures of reliability and quality. They're in the enviable position of gaining market share in a growing market. Your customers want their customers to be happy, content with the price and performance of their offerings. Your job is to help them achieve that goal.

Bear in mind that business acumen is not a matter of being able to calculate numbers to the ninth decimal place. The idea is to pull the basic numbers from the customer's financial reports and other public documents, to look at them in combination and compare with previous years and future projections. You do not have to be a financial expert to get a picture of what's changing and in what direction. And the more you do it, the better you'll get.

How to Communicate with the Customer

While you're searching for answers to your growing lists of questions about the customer, you also need to begin establishing a way for your company and your customer to communicate. A weekly sales call on the purchasing manager isn't what I'm talking about here. Instead, you need to establish multiple contacts between your company and your customer so that functional people know one another and can come together quickly and easily to solve problems or clear roadblocks. Your lawyers, for example, should be talking to your customer's lawyers about the forms contracts may take so that when the time comes to actually sign on the dotted line there won't be last minute misunderstandings or changes. Similarly, your credit people need to establish good relations now with your customer's treasurer's office so that credit approval is done long before a deal is made and the terms of payment can be incorporated when possible into the solution you devise for your customer.

The final step to ensure long lasting and profitable customer relations is to incorporate post-sale servicing into the overall process. The sale does not end when the contract is signed. It is the customer's experience—and, in many cases, the experience of the customer's customer— that develops the long-term relationship. Only if the customer is satisfied that he has received all that was promised, and that the solution does indeed address his financial concerns, have you succeeded. And that success is not an end unto itself, but rather just another step in a long journey of working with your customer to continue to solve problems and develop new approaches to doing business together.

Finally, you must always remember your responsibility to protect the knowledge a customer-partner is sharing with you. Information flow is the key to trust. Don't abuse it.

4

The Value Account Plan

Several months into the change effort, Charlie, who had lost that all-important sale to Progis Corporation, had another chance with another large client, TriNet Inc. Charlie was the team leader on the project. He was in the midst of preparing the guts of the presentation, which was slated for a week from Wednesday. But as he got deeper into it, he realized that he was missing some vital pieces of information.

For example, while he had a good deal of data on the company's industry, its competitive dynamics, and its sales growth pattern, he realized that he did not really know which manager in TriNet would make the final buying decision. Was it the purchasing manager? Probably not, he realized, recalling the way events played out when he went up against Progis. Was it the CFO or the head of marketing? Perhaps the executive vice president of manufacturing? He had to admit that he simply didn't know.

In addition, while Charlie felt that he had a pretty

good idea about what the final offering would look like, he realized that he had no idea what to charge for it. He had heard a lot about "premium pricing" in recent weeks, but he did not know how to figure out what to charge for his "new and enhanced" product offering. He was afraid to charge himself out of the sale. He had gotten mixed signals from finance. They were accustomed to charging cost plus a percentage, but he was told they "no longer did things that way."

He realized that he had a long way to go before he and the team would be ready to present anything, and he had scheduled a run-through for Friday. Suddenly he felt the same kind of panic he felt when he lost that big sale several months back. He realized that things were changing much faster than he realized, and unless he kept up, he would be transformed into a dinosaur in his industry.

That realization was followed by another: he wasn't in it alone. He had lots of people in the company he could call on to plug the holes, many of whom had been talking regularly with people at the customer's shop. He also reminded himself that the point was not to make the sale at any cost but to build rapport with the customer, to develop trust, and to learn more about the business.

His nerves calmed as he picked up the phone to assemble the team for some last minute analysis and clarification. He would then commit to paper a summary of the customer's needs and opportunities and the value proposition Sturgis was prepared to deliver. He would have to be prepared to explain that the value to the customer goes beyond cost reduction to include new ideas for helping the company reach its revenue growth and cash generation goals.

The last thing a salesperson needs is more paperwork. But here's a document no company should be without: a *value account plan,* or VAP. A VAP is the name I use for the document that defines the value proposition and the business benefits the customer can expect to get from it. Those benefits must be expressed in business terms: in quantitative measures such as cost reduction, revenue growth, and cash flow improvement, and qualitative measures such as sustainable market share and brand image. Translating the customer's needs into a unique offering with well-defined business benefits is the crucial distinction between value creation selling and the traditional approach. The VAP provides the road map to make that translation and is the central tool of this new approach to selling.

A VAP is a template, on a computer or on paper, that the salesperson must complete with the help of her colleagues in other functions. But it is not something that can be filled out mechanically because it is the quality of the insights that matters. The VAP demands a great deal of thinking. It forces the team to go beyond what they already know and what the customer tells them to define offerings that provide business benefits customers may not realize they need. It prompts the team to collaborate in using the comprehensive information they've gathered about the customer, then to think more broadly about the customer's business and to create a value proposition that helps that business thrive. The mental work that goes into creating the VAP turns the gathering of information into valuable intellectual capital.

The salesperson takes the lead in galvanizing a multidisciplinary team to analyze customer information and build the VAP. Once complete, the VAP is the centerpiece around which the company collaborates. It is a shared document that is accessible to the appropriate people throughout your company and thus provides focus and continuity, even if key members of the sales team leave or get promoted.

Some salespeople may feel the VAP reduces their importance, but in fact they have an elevated role in overseeing it, filling it in, and using it to shape irresistible value propositions for their customers. Despite any initial resistance, they will soon find the VAP to be the most useful tool in their drawer.

You won't be able to order off-the-shelf software for your VAP. Companies undertaking value creation selling have created their own versions tailored to their customers, their organizations, and their industries. Some have cobbled together their own software applications, while others use a printed form. You too will have to create your own VAP. That won't be hard to do once you understand the basic outline of what a VAP should contain and how you will use it.

Every VAP should include three elements: a concise description, or snapshot, of the customer; a value proposition; and the benefits the value proposition gives to the customer expressed in physical terms—such as "improving cycle time by X minutes" or "cutting inventories by X dollars"—and in business terms—such as cost, revenue, profit margin, cash, ROI, market share, and brand equity.

Value Proposition Account Plan

Customer Snap Shot

- Basic information and contacts
- Total picture of the Customer business
- Decision making in the Customer shop

Value Proposition

Customer need	Your offerings	Your financials
Scope	product A	your Price
Timing	product B	cost
Physical needs	Service C	Profit
	Unique integration	Capital Investment

Benefit to the Customer (T.V.O.)

Year	Physical Benefits	margins	Cash flow	Revenue growth	RoI	Brand Equity	Market share	Qualitative Shifts	Remarks
0-1									
2-3									
3+									

Customer Snapshot

The first of three major components of a VAP is a concise description of the customer. In preparation for the VAP, you will have collected a ton of information about the customer, as described in Chapter 3. That is the raw material for creating the VAP. You should begin by recording the basics: the company's name, line or lines of business, information about the location of headquarters and subsidiaries, and names of senior executives.

Then the intellectual work begins. The salesperson takes the lead by enlisting the help of her colleagues to sift out the important facts to create a clear, concise picture of the customer's total business. The team has to broaden its scope to look at the big picture of the customer's business—its financial picture, competitive dynamics, goals, markets, operations, and its entire value chain (see page 8). You can't take things at face value but should do your own creative thinking to discern the reality of the customer's business, boiling it down to the essentials. This is the time to consider impressions and perceptions and make some judgments.

If, for instance, you have a customer's financial data for the past five years, your own financial executives can analyze them, looking for important shifts. They might see that one customer's shrinking margins, combined with its very high debt structure in a rising interest rate and tight-money environment, are pointing to an imminent squeeze on cash. The customer has proclaimed it will be growing fast, but you might conclude otherwise.

Another customer might be gaining financial strength and building its cash. You can combine that insight with other information, perhaps noting that the particular market segments the customer has targeted are growing, and that competitors are struggling. All of this should be recorded in brief language and used to shape the value proposition.

You might have learned the customer's stated short-term and long-term goals. Short-term goals tend to be realistic, and if they're not, they usually get adjusted pretty quickly. But a customer's long-term goals might be pie in the sky, adjusted only incrementally over time until finally it becomes clear that they will not be achieved. That's when the company might make an abrupt move, radically changing its goals and strategic direction. If you track how well or poorly the customer is moving toward its goals, you might be able to predict the possibility of a radical shift.

The customer snapshot also should include information about the customer's decision makers. Decisions seldom are made at one sitting or by one person. You want to ferret out *who* makes the decisions, *what* or *who* influences the decisions, and *how* they make those decisions. On whose budget in the customer shop will the cost and benefits appear? How is it changing? Is it clear, or do you need to search for additional pieces of the puzzle?

You can capture this snapshot as a set of bullet points or paragraphs—whatever form works best for you—keeping in mind that businesses are in constant flux. You will have to keep this updated by watching for changes in people, relationships, and organizational structure at the purchasing level and throughout the organization.

Customer Snap shot
_____

- Basic Information and Contacts

- Total picture of The customer's business

- Decision making in The customer's shop.

The Value Proposition

The second part of the VAP is the value proposition. Here you define the customer need you will meet, the mix of offerings customized to that customer, its pricing, and its implications for your own company's revenues, cost, cash, capital investment, and profitability. Creating a value proposition may seem like familiar ground. What's different here is that the VAP forces you to think about your customer's total business and to tap the best thinking of people from many parts of your company to come up with a value proposition that provides benefits to the customer beyond the usual cost savings.

One of the greatest hurdles for salespeople new to value creation selling is reaching people other than their traditional contacts in purchasing and getting their attention right away. There are no formulas for doing this, but companies who take this approach to selling do develop methods for making contacts, networking, and getting the information they need. It is often a matter of brainstorming who at your company might have a social or professional connection with someone in the customer's business, and being aggressive in connecting with that person. We live in a relational society, so chances are somebody knows somebody. You increase the odds when you network with multiple functions and hierarchical levels at your company. Also, a salesperson can ask the people she already knows in the customer's shop who her colleagues should get to know. As salespeople and their colleagues find ways to engage in frequent dialogue with the customer, they can use those contacts to create a value proposition that addresses needs and priorities beyond the purchasing department.

Say your customer is a consumer goods company that buys packaging from you. The purchasing person is interested primarily in the price or cost of the package and the reliability of delivery and quality. But the marketing person in the same customer organization is interested in how the packaging affects the use of shelf space at the retailer and whether it reinforces or enhances the brand. A senior leader or public relations executive in the same company is concerned about sustainability and being "green." Knowing all that, you might create a value proposition to provide a package that is recyclable, is consistent with the brand in terms of aesthetics and quality, makes efficient use of shelf space, and can be purchased economically. Such a value proposition would be appealing to many people in the customer's organization, including high-level executives, who might weigh in on the decision. It would have greater value to the customer's business.

Formulating a successful solution for a customer

requires the involvement of more than one silo. People have to share and debate, particularly horizontally, what is available or possible, and then commit to it. If you are just bundling together existing products you probably won't produce a real value-creating solution. In fact, if you bundle the products together the customer often will be able to separate the components and price them separately, then demand discounts. Then you've gone backward. For the value proposition to be unique, the sales leader has to demand that his team figure out how to integrate the package in a customized way that creates value and differentiates the solution from what the competition can offer. That would make value creation more than the sum of its parts.

You also have to figure out the pricing and cost information early on, to make the customer benefits concrete and to ensure that the plan makes money for your company. Pricing has to be customized for each customer and for each solution using your company's best expertise. Pricing is where many companies let their sales force down. If the solution is right, you can break away from cost-plus pricing and charge a premium price.

A company that is selling value-creating solutions uses value pricing, which is different. Value pricing means you have to calculate the total value to the customer of what you're going to offer. Then you have to estimate, using your best judgment, what the competition is going to offer. What is their ability to have a smart solution and how will they price it? How does the customer view your proposed solution and how well does the customer understand the value of your solution? See if that pricing leaves you enough on the table to continue further. Unless you change your approval process for pricing your value proposition, value creation selling won't work. Value pricing demonstrates to the customer that the pie will increase for both his company and yours, and it becomes a matter of determining how to slice the pie. In transactional selling the salesperson feels responsible for the performance of the product. In shaping the VAP, the sales leader feels responsible for the customer's business outcome.

Salespeople may have a psychological blockage about premium pricing. They are used to customers driving hard on price—and losing deals because of it. As they get more comfortable shaping value propositions that meet multiple business needs, they will see that premium pricing is indeed warranted, and that customers are more than willing to accept it. Finance people might also resist the concept of value pricing because it requires more judgment than cost-plus pricing, but as your people become adept in defining the business benefits beyond cost savings, it will all make sense.

Value Proposition

Customer need	Your Offerings	Your Financials
• Scope	• Product A	Your Price
• Timing	• Product B	• Cost
• Physical needs	• Service C	• Profit
	• Unique integration	• Capital Investment

The Business Benefits

The third part of the VAP defines the benefits of the value proposition. At most companies, sales agents are accustomed to thinking about value in terms of the customer's total cost of ownership, or TCO, which includes the cost of the purchase and any expenses associated with using it; then they compare that to the potential savings. But this third part of the VAP is built to determine the TVO—the total *value* of ownership. TVO is an estimate of all the benefits the customer stands to gain as well as what he might lose if he chooses to go another way. In industries where innovation is occurring rapidly customers who buy strictly on price, not total value, are at a competitive disadvantage and will fall behind.

You must first state the physical benefits of your value proposition: billing errors are cut in half, for example, or raw material consumption is reduced by 20 percent. Then you define and quantify all the business benefits of the solution. Some will be quantitative; these will include any cost savings, but also any projected gains in revenue, margin or cash flow, and market share. Other benefits will be qualitative, such as better customer retention and an improved brand image. You have to think through the benefits of your value proposition and be comfortable making judgments about them, bearing in mind that benefits such as revenue growth and brand enhancement are of real value to customers.

Say a software supplier can increase the number of sales calls a pharmaceutical company's reps make on doctors each week. Increasing the number of sales calls from 10 to 15 per person per week is the physical benefit; it's what the solution actually *does*. But if each of those five additional sales calls produces an average of $5,000 in revenue, the physical benefit translates into an additional $25,000 in revenue per salesperson per week. Multiply that $25,000 by fifty-two weeks in the year and you get $1.3 million. Now multiply that $1.3 million times one thousand sales reps and you discover that the customer stands to gain $1.3 billion in additional annual revenue by using the software. That number is sure to attract the interest of top management. It is a specific benefit to the customer's business that can be quantified and measured over time. The software might also provide some qualitative benefits, such as increased customer satisfaction and improved brand image. All of these would be listed in the VAP and factored into the customer's TVO.

Keep in mind that although sales agents can rely on their colleagues for help translating the physical benefits into financial language, they will have to hone their business acumen. Thinking through how a physical benefit will make their customer's business perform better is the crux of their job in value creation selling. They will also be expected to understand the basics of income statements and balance sheets, which were laid out in Chapter 3, "Developing Your Business Acumen."

Remember that when reduced to the basics, business is largely common sense. It can be learned through practice, preferably under the guidance of leaders whose business acumen is well developed. The fact is, some salespeople are learning it, so we know it can be done. Those who practice using business acumen in creating a VAP will indeed get better at it. Ultimately, they'll win more business on the basis of facts, quantification, solid business reasoning, and their definition of customer need than on the basis of personal persuasion or relationships alone.

Probing for more information about the customer's business will help you spot customer benefits you might otherwise miss. Take the case of Thomson Financial, one of several players providing software aimed at traders in the financial markets. Its software allowed traders to find and display market information almost instantaneously—but so did competitors' products. The IT purchasers, finding little to differentiate the products, negotiated heavily on the price of the software. But as Thomson embraced value creation selling, it put a fundamental question to its salespeople: Are you clear and very specific about what the customer needs, how the product is to be used and how it benefits the customer? This prompted people at Thomson to distinguish between the IT departments that were the *purchasers* of its software products and the traders who were the *users*. People at Thomson began to carefully observe and talk to the users. They found that while instantaneous access to market information was useful to the traders, the real benefit was that the software gave them the ability to manipulate all the information and juxtapose it to gain insights into market dynamics, and thus make better decisions. Thomson's software was improving not only the traders' *efficiency* but also their *effectiveness,* a much more valuable feature than mere speed of display. Making better decisions is difficult to measure in dollar terms, but the users know it makes a qualitative difference in their business.

You will get even more ideas if you look at the whole

value chain, from the consumer or retail chain backward. When MeadWestvaco did that for its new packaging concept, Natralock, a tear-resistant paperboard package aimed at replacing the so-called clamshell packages, it identified a range of benefits for its consumer goods customers. Like the clamshell packages, Natralock would prevent theft, but it would also provide great graphics and was more environmentally friendly. A key benefit, though, fell to consumers: the Natralock package is easier to open. MeadWestvaco's solution helps its customers boost revenue because they can provide a package consumers would prefer.

Although I've described the three parts of the VAP sequentially, they require you to go through them iteratively. Efforts to define the benefits might push you to learn more about your customer, and defining the benefits goes hand in hand with shaping the value proposition, particularly regarding price. Understanding the TVO is crucial to value pricing.

The MeadWestvaco sales force, working with Coca-Cola, learned that there is value to be gained in the quality of the printing on a carton of Coke. Higher-quality printing has a direct correlation with shelf turnover and brand image. If MeadWestvaco can bring to Coca-Cola a higher-quality package, Coke will get better inventory turns and brand image, both of which are measurable. MeadWestvaco will stand a better chance to get premium pricing on its solution than a competitor.

Remember that when the benefits fall on multiple areas of the customer's business, there may be bigger budgets to tap as well. An innovative packaging solution might come partly from the customer's packaging budget, for instance, and partly from the marketing budget, which sees advantages at the point of purchase.

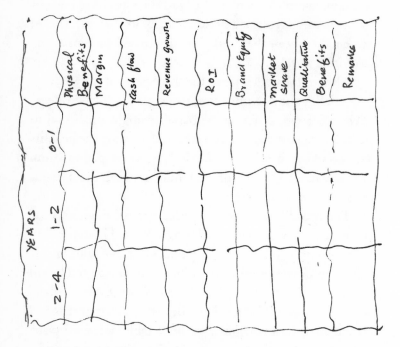

Benefits to the Customer

T.V.O (Total value of ownership)

Salesperson as Team Leader

Creating the VAP is a team effort led by the sales leaders, who pull people together from across many functional silos and get them engaged with the customer and with each other. Social relationships between the selling organization and the customer are important, but so are relationships among the functions at your own company. As team leaders, salespeople play a crucial role in shaping them, ensuring that people talk often and openly.

In value creation selling, people in many parts of your business are expected to build relationships with their counterparts in the customer shop. The sales leader has to get those people together to share the information they've gathered and help interpret it. As the group pinpoints the customer's needs and talks about what they could offer to meet them, the sales leader must be skilled in drawing out people's ideas and commitments. Each functional silo has its own priorities, budget constraints, and targets, which can become obstacles in providing a value proposition to the customer. The leader has to get people to shift their focus to the common goal of providing an attractive solution, so they are willing to make appropriate trade-offs. When they contribute to the VAP in this way, they are more committed to their role in helping deliver on it.

Delivering a value proposition for its consumer goods customers using Natralock, for instance, required commitments from many parts of MeadWestvaco. First, developing and manufacturing Natralock took a large, sustained investment, which operations and finance had to be willing to make. Resources had to shift, as did mindsets. Marketing had to support the new product launch, and salespeople had to become consultants to their customers to communicate the value of MeadWestvaco's clamshell alternative. Because the whole thing was revolutionary, everyone had to be willing to work through the challenges in developing it. MeadWestvaco succeeded because a cross-functional team participated in the solution, knew the potential benefits for customers and consumers, and were committed to making it work. They met regularly to measure progress and shift resources to address any problems that arose. It wasn't a matter of sales imposing a solution that operations was expected to deliver on and finance was supposed to fund, and later discovering roadblocks in those areas.

To a great extent you're doing in your own shop what you've also been doing in your customer's shop: learning as much as you can about the operation, the problems, and the people. You're sharing information about the customer with people throughout your company and getting their reactions and thoughts about how the relationship between the two companies can be improved and what can be done to help the customer.

That's not to say that you won't encounter obstacles in working on the VAP. Someone may well say that something can't be done, when in fact it can. The sales leader has to be the advocate for the customer, clearly visualizing what the solution could look like, pushing others to do the same, but at the same time listening to the real-world constraints others identify. That's why the team may have to go through iterations, revising the value proposition based on ongoing dialogue with the customer and people back home. As people work together on the VAP, pooling their expertise about what is possible and generating ideas, they improve their social relationships, enhancing the coordination and flow of information throughout the company.

All the people within your company who take a hand in analyzing the customer, diagnosing his problems and crafting a solution become part of the "sales team." At a financial company, you're drawing on your experts in mergers and acquisitions, derivatives, and the like to shape an offering for a client. At a machinery company, you might be exploring with your engineers whether a new motor design can make your old machines more energy-efficient, and talking with others about whether you can loan the customer one of the bigger models for a 30-day test.

The sales force should always have immediate access to finance for credit analysis and to legal in order to expedite contracts. The aim is to always move faster than the competition in meeting customer needs. EDS maintained a dashboard of key items on four hundred customers 24/7. The customer could directly log a complaint and EDS would immediately seek the cause and fix it. The sales force could devote its efforts to selling problem resolutions. Of course, if there is no internal structure for dealing quickly and thoroughly with complaints, the dashboard won't work.

Similarly, as you open the dialogue on the customer side, you will get some of the same benefits. Often in preparing the VAP you have to go back to customers to clarify their needs and get more insight into how you can translate those needs into business language. There will be lots of back-and-forth to answer questions and test out ideas. When you're working toward the customer's best interest, they will find this involvement helpful, not harassing. The more you can demonstrate that you're engaging them as a partner in defining their need and shaping a solution, and not just dumping a solution on their desk, the more open the interaction will become. The social structure between your company and the customer's, and maybe even within the customer's organization, improves.

The VAP becomes increasingly detailed and accurate, and your customers become a great source of ideas and innovations that will fuel their—and your—continued growth.

It takes time to build the trust and two-way flow of information that are your ultimate goal. In your first attempts to do a VAP and the various forms it might take you may be working without your customer's collaboration. But regardless of whether your customer is an active participant, you need to be the leader who pulls together the relevant information and people to complete the VAP to be presented to your customer.

What you're striving for is an organization that does what Wick Jones used to do personally. You've probably never had heard of Wick Jones, but in the packaging industry he's something of a legend. When he ran R. A. Jones Company, the family company he inherited, he used his personal relationships with customers and knowledge of his company's capabilities to forge unique solutions that kept customers coming back—at times, even pleading—for more. Jones was on a first-name basis with the chieftains at P&G, Kellogg, General Mills, Anheuser-Busch, and many other giant companies that bought his company's packaging equipment, and relished the times when he would sit with them over a drink or dinner and brainstorm ideas for their business.

On one such occasion, when Jones was talking with August Busch in St. Louis, he learned that Busch had come to the conclusion that all the millions of dollars the company was spending on advertising only increased awareness of the product. Actual decision making was at the point-of-purchase, where graphics and packaging drove the sale. Jones knew that Busch understood consumer behavior well and took it upon himself to help him drive incremental sales of beer through point-of-purchase packaging.

Jones, who was always focused on the customer's need, not what his company's technical people wanted to provide, took that information back to his company. He got people together to figure out how they might design some equipment to improve the package design, and thus boost Anheuser-Busch's sales. The technical people figured out how to make customized machinery that allowed Anheuser-Busch to sell a pack of 35 cans of beer with attractive graphics at the same price as Miller's 28-packs. It would take 12 to 14 months for Miller to reproduce that package size, and because brand loyalty is important for beer drinkers, that lead was extended.

In devising the solution, Jones didn't just talk to the engineers who designed the machinery. He involved people from the manufacturing floor, who often could anticipate problems in producing a piece of equipment and come up with practical ways around them. They would have to make the equipment. He also made sure the sales and service people were on board.

Jones did this routinely for many customers, who so appreciated Jones's contribution to their business that they often asked him to work with them. In one case, General Mills approached Jones for help with a new kind of cereal bag Wal-Mart wanted them to use, but Jones didn't want to take it on. General Mills turned to a new supplier, but the machines had a lot of problems. One of the executives from General Mills said later that every time he walked by one of them, he thought to himself, "If

Jones had taken on this project, it would have been done right, and we'd be selling more product."

Creating a VAP

In 2005, a cross-functional team of people at MeadWestvaco pulled together to see if they could win new business by customizing a value proposition to help a targeted customer solve a business problem. The team started by gathering everything they knew about the potential customer and enlisted the help of third parties to study the customer's market and consumers' buying behavior.

The targeted customer sold restaurant-quality ethnic frozen foods to retail and club store outlets. It was a midsize niche player competing against some very big players, such as Nestle, ConAgra, and Tyson, differentiating itself on the basis of the quality and freshness of the ingredients it used. It had developed a distinctive packaging design to reinforce its premium positioning and pricing. But some of the packages were getting damaged after delivery to the supermarkets and couldn't be sold. The rate of "unsalables" was rising, and one of the biggest chains was threatening to reduce freezer space. Waste and cost were not the only problems posed by unsalables. A study MeadWestvaco commissioned to examine consumers' reactions to damaged goods in a retail environment found that shoppers would pass over the damaged packages most of the time, and worse, that the images of the product, the customer's brand, and the retailer were negatively affected.

That study was just part of the extensive research MeadWestvaco did. MeadWestvaco also made a thorough assessment of the frozen-foods industry, breaking it down into segments and making growth projections, segment by segment, based on historical trends. MeadWestvaco found, for instance, that while the frozen-foods market overall was not growing much, the ethnic foods segment, particularly at the premium end, was. The customer stood to miss this growth if it couldn't stem the rise of unsalables. MeadWestvaco also did a breakdown of the customer's money making. Specific numbers were not available because the customer was privately owned, but the team extrapolated from similar companies in the same category to estimate costs, inventory turns, and margins.

MeadWestvaco used its research to demonstrate that it understood the customer's business problem—and then solved it. It created a package using a specific kind of paperboard called Coated Natural Kraft® (CNK), which could take on high-impact graphics and still had the structural integrity to prevent package damage. Those characteristics met the customer's physical needs, but the team at MeadWestvaco knew that wasn't enough. They had to get the customer to look beyond the unit price of its product by presenting the panoply of business benefits, which included increased revenues, improved cash flow by reducing inventories for the retailer, reduced unsalables and returns, protected market position and sales level, protected brand equity, and sustained consumer loyalty. Each of these benefits was backed up with facts and data.

All of that became part of the VAP that guided Mead-Westvaco's selling efforts. It allowed the team to show that despite the higher unit price, the reduction in damage made switching to MeadWestvaco's CNK package financially beneficial. At the same time, better packaging would

VAP

Abbreviated

Value chain

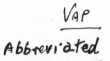

Meadwest Vaco   Brand x   Retailer   Consumer

Old ———————————————→

New ←———————————————

VALUE PROPOSITION

CUSTOMER NEED

- Frozen Food Packaging material
- Causes unsaleables in retail outlets
- 75% of shoppers push a damaged package to the side.
- Brand perception drops from 70% to 41% with even a slight damage.

VAP continued

- Your offering
- CNK (TM) - a special packaging material - trade marked
- Reduces unsakables by 40% or more
- Retailer's shelf space utilization goes up
- Brand perception improves

. . . .

- Benefits to the customer (TVO)

Physical Benefits	Margins	Cash flow	ROI	Brand Equity	Market share
Reduction in unsakeables	· Up · Food is not Wasted	Up · Less Inventory	Up	brand perception is Up	Up · Revenues are growing

help the customer secure a position and gain shelf space with warehouse clubs and other big retailers. The team used similar analysis to show how the retailer (the customer's customer) would benefit, thus giving the targeted customer ideas for how to sell its products more effectively.

Getting the customer to focus on revenue growth, not just cost, was a major shift in thinking. MeadWestvaco won the sale and, ultimately more important, the customer's trust and respect.

5

Developing the Value Creation Sales Force

Three months after the off-site meeting, Rob Morris, the western district regional manager for Sturgis, ran into Jack Garrett, the CEO, in the company cafeteria. Jack invited Rob to join him for lunch.

"So how are things going?" Jack asked enthusiastically.

Rob knew how important the initiative was to Jack—and to the company. He avoided eye contact when he replied that the transformation wasn't going all that well. "It's certainly not happening as quickly as I would like," he admitted.

"It can't be that bad," Jack replied. "What's the problem?"

"My reps are having a hard time pulling together all of the information we talked about at the off-site. One of their biggest complaints is that they can't reach the people they need to reach in the customer's shop. Their primary contacts are fighting them tooth and nail, trying to keep control of the buying process."

"I had a feeling that might happen," Jack said. "Are the reps getting help from other departments at Sturgis?"

"To be honest, Jack, some of our reps don't like working as part of a team. They're not accustomed to reaching out to other departments, and they don't like sharing everything with people in other parts of the company.

"But most of them are coming around," Rob continued. "In part because they're realizing they can't complete a VAP without help. Getting past the physical product and translating the benefits into something beyond cost reduction is a challenge."

"That's the toughest part," Jack acknowledged. "But it's central to their job. This kind of selling is a big shift and it'll take practice. But it's a shift they have to make. They've got to work at it. That's why I'm planning to raise the level of training to certification level."

"What do you mean, 'certification level'?" Rob interrupted.

"I mean they'll have to pass an exam at the end of the training program."

"That's not going to go over well with many of . . ."

"Rob, we don't have a choice," Jack said sharply. "And time isn't on our side. Every day we do things the old way we lose an opportunity to differentiate ourselves in the eyes of our customers. That's a prescription for failure. We have to change and do it quickly or we risk being made irrelevant in the marketplace. We've got to face up to the fact that it takes a different mind-set and different skills to do this. We can provide support, but we've also got to be prepared to sort out the people who can't make the transition."

"You're right. You can count on me to help get the urgency across. I'll do whatever it takes to win," Rob said emphatically.

"I know, Rob, and many thanks."

Suspecting that other regions were facing similar issues, Jack quickly arranged to meet with Susan, the executive vice president of sales. Susan confirmed that the western region was struggling, but she also had some good news. She told Jack that at least two regional managers had a firm grasp of value creation selling, and she knew half a dozen salespeople who also seemed to get it. They had already made headway with two big customers who were ready to sit down with a sales team to explore how Sturgis could help them boost their market share and revenues.

Jack was glad to hear that the new process was catching on in at least a few territories. "Let's get some of those people to present at our next training session," he suggested. "They can show everyone else that we can make this change and have fun doing it."

"I've got just the person," Susan said. "Charlie Baldwin. He pulled me aside the other day to tell me he feels like the wind is back in his sail. He was beginning to think he couldn't book a sale to save his life, but now he's reenergized. He's become one of our biggest champions."

"Put the right tools in the hands of someone like Charlie," Jack replied, "and we're sure to succeed."

Make no mistake about it, a concerted effort to create a value creation sales force simply cannot succeed without two critical elements: buy-in and extensive training. An individual salesperson who "gets it" can make headway by personally reshaping relationships with customers and throughout her own organization. But senior leaders who want to adopt value creation selling companywide should approach it at a deliberate pace and realize that it is not an overnight process. The company cannot stop what it is doing to make the transition. Instead it has to be done on the fly, much like changing a tire on a car moving 60 miles an hour. It will take time to make the transition from the old way of doing business, and the larger the organization is, the longer that transition will take.

The best way to adopt VCS is to start by selecting a few salespeople who have the skills and personal attributes to understand and execute the new approach. They should be people who are willing to change their psychology and mind-set from "doing deals" to ensuring that their customer is successful. Great transactional salespeople are not necessarily the kind of businesspeople VCS demands.

The most promising individuals should be trained and assigned to a select set of clients that seem receptive to the new way of doing business. As this initial contingent begins to enjoy some early and visible successes, word will spread and other salespeople will become more enthusiastic about making the change. At the same time, those who are resistant to the change and either can't or won't embrace it will become more obvious. They may be susceptible to counsel and encouragement and eventually come around. If not, they will either opt out of their own accord or have to be moved to another position in the company or replaced. Companies that have undertaken VCS find that anywhere from a third to a half of their original sales force can and are willing to do value creation selling. If you consider that half your sales force may not adapt to the new approach, it is apparent that your transition has to be thoughtful and done at the right speed.

It goes without saying that sales managers must be enthusiastic supporters of the transformation, and they too must learn new skills. Other functional leaders must change too, demonstrating their own enthusiasm and willingness to collaborate with the sales force.

The Right Stuff

Value creation selling does indeed require a new breed of salesperson, and you should take the time to clarify what traits and skills the new breed should have. While no one person will embody all of them, anyone in the role of sales team leader should exhibit at least some of the fundamentals.

Here is what Brian Parke of Unifi, the North Carolina textile company, says about recruiting new salespeople into a VCS culture:

> If we were hiring a salesperson today we would be very careful to get the right educational level, the right profile. We would look for someone who is sociable, articulate, and very competitive. We would want somebody who understands business. He could be a classics major or a business major as

long as the person understands how to make money. He or she doesn't have to come from the Ivy League—he could be the product of a local college. In the end, we would look for someone who can solve problems, because at the end of the day you're trying to solve customers' problems.

Thomson Financial, like Unifi, has been implementing a value creation selling strategy for a few years now. Here is how they describe the attributes of a sales team leader:

The new sales team leader is a generalist. The leader is a highly intelligent and skilled listener and is unusually disciplined. He or she is able to conceptualize the business as well as the needs, work flow, and processes of the customer in the customer's language. The leader has a business mind and knows the customer's market and industry segments well. He or she is able to conceptualize solutions for the customer and makes sure the solutions work for the customer. The leader is a great communicator who knows how to overcome objections and can make excellent and persuasive presentations. He or she is an integrator who can move cross-functionally and across boundaries easily and is excellent in mobilizing the right and timely resources from within and outside the organization. He or she knows and practices the art of relationship building. This is a new breed for many companies.

Clayton LiaBraaten, a senior vice president of marketing and sales for INFONXX North America, which sells sophisticated telephone services such as directory assistance, contact center services, and speech recognition, describes the type of sales leader needed for VCS as a "harvester" rather than a purely transaction-oriented "hunter" whose instinct is to move on after striking a deal:

> In our business, there's room for both. But as we've shifted our sales approach to emphasize deeper, longer-term customer engagements, we've started looking for more people who are harvesters. These are the people who stay involved and accessible to customers, have exquisite diplomacy skills, and stay calm under fire. They're effective in managing across internal functions and know how to balance transparency with protecting confidences on both sides. We even changed the job title from account manager to account developer to signal that we expect those people to be actively engaged with the customer at all times, not just when fires erupt.

The following list of skills and traits may help you develop your own methods for determining people's suitability, strengths, and weaknesses.

Affability. In VCS, it is not sufficient to have a hail-fellow-well-met attitude. Since most customers or buying organizations have decision-making units involving more than one person from more than one department and from more than one level, the value creation selling salesperson must establish a social network within the customer's organization. At the same time, the salesperson must establish a similar network within her own company. The salesperson must be a great communicator who listens and distills what she hears and can jointly explore the issues. She becomes the point person linking the two organizations, moving seamlessly between them to define the customer's problems and goals and to help her own company devise an appropriate solution.

Conceptualizing Problems and Solutions. This is the ability to sift through large amounts of seemingly unrelated data to generate alternative ideas about offerings that work for both the customer and the seller. Once the necessary information has been extracted from the customer and shared in the selling organization, the salesperson has to identify specifically what the customer needs and how her own organization can link its processes with the customer's processes to create value for the customer. The salesperson must think creatively to come up with an offering that has demonstrable, concrete benefits for the customer, but at the same time earns an appropriate profit and beats the competition.

Leadership. Not to be confused with personal charisma or heroic efforts, the kind of leadership the salesperson needs to demonstrate is the ability to manage a team of people over whom he has little or no hierarchical authority. There will be instances, for example, when members of the sales team outrank the salesperson. The leader cannot be intimidated. This leadership ability may not be easy to spot at first, but it will become evident over time by how the team is built, how the sales leader conducts the dialogue, how frequent and productive the meetings are, and how she seeks and obtains collaboration. A leader should be able to facilitate dialogue between the seller and the customer, and get others involved to suggest ideas, devise solutions, and make decisions faster, better, and deeper than the competition. That must be done while keeping profitable revenue growth in sight. Lone-wolf salespeople often have trouble leading a group effort.

Tenacity. The type and depth of customer information necessary for VCS is not easy to obtain. While some information can be derived from published documents and databases, the most important information comes from multiple levels of the customer's organization and from the customer's customers, who often cannot clearly articulate their own needs or goals. Extracting that kind of information takes extensive effort and time. Not all salespeople are willing to accept the delays. Even after a lot of information is extracted from the customer, it must then be distributed and analyzed back home, where you'll discover you need even more. The process of gathering data and going through iterations of the value proposition can seem never-ending. Salespeople must have the patience and tenacity to keep driving the team and the process.

Business Acumen. The most difficult aspect of VCS is understanding the customer's business and its processes, all expressed in the language of business that I discussed earlier. Salespeople should be able to dissect a profit-and-loss statement, a balance sheet, and the relationship between them and feel psychologically comfortable doing that.

You may have to create internal courses to teach these skills. Further, because the kind of information needed to create a value proposition resides in different places within complex, fast-moving organizations, the person must be familiar with the basic language of various departments.

Training from the Top

Making the transition to VCS requires new behaviors as well as specific new skills. Training is essential. Representatives from various support functions, particularly finance, legal, marketing, and product development, should be trained, but by far the greatest need for training will be the sales force.

Ideally, training the sales force will start at the top, beginning with the executive vice president of sales or whoever has the equivalent title. He or she must demonstrate the ability to extract information, complete a VAP, and formulate a solution. After that, training proceeds down to the level of regional sales managers, who have to gain expertise as well. They should be prepared to shape value propositions around a broad set of business goals so they can spread the pilot program throughout the company. The CEO should be sure that the head of sales and regional managers master VCS and take ownership for training and certifying others. Tying a sizable portion—say, 40 percent—of their incentive pay to implementing VCS can ensure those leaders take it seriously.

Training the entire sales force is a huge undertaking that cannot—and should not—be done overnight. It's best to start with some carefully selected salespeople who you think will do well with VCS. Selecting the right people to start with is key, especially because you will want to be able to leverage your early successes.

The first contingent of salespeople to undergo training should exhibit not only classical sales skills, such as affability and high energy, but also an eagerness to learn new skills, imagination and perceptiveness, and some leadership traits. Perhaps there are a few salespeople with business degrees who already have some business acumen. Reviewing resumes might reveal a few more salespeople who demonstrated leadership abilities sometime in the past, perhaps in college as president of the student body or quarterback of the football team.

The decision about who to train first should be considered in conjunction with deciding which accounts to target for the new sales approach. Since the value creation selling strategy will be implemented incrementally over time, a company can start with just a few accounts. These accounts can act as vehicles for training. They should be customers with whom your company already has a collaborative relationship and ones where you think your company could make a significant contribution.

Don't be fooled by age. Many managers consider young people to be more malleable and enthusiastic about change, but older salespeople may find the new approach energizing and become eager to master the new skills that are necessary. Lou Eccleston, the former president of global sales, marketing and services at Thomson Financial, found that resilience and flexibility were the hallmarks of salespeople making a successful transition to VCS.

"It isn't like the young people get it and the older ones don't," says Eccleston. "Some of our most valuable people are the ones who have been here a long time. And it isn't about type A personalities or anything like that. It really comes down to whether a person is excited by choice, change, and growth versus stability and safety."

The best situation would be to find qualified salespeople who are already servicing the accounts you want to penetrate more deeply, although you might have to switch assignments.

The Building Blocks of Training

Training for VCS must make salespeople aware of the new skills they need and help them practice those skills. PowerPoint presentations, the basis of most training today, is not sufficient. VCS is such a major change for experienced salespeople, who have been conditioned to think and act in certain ways, that it takes tremendous rigor to rearrange the synapses in the brain. Case studies and intense practice are more effective. Discussing real cases, sharing insights from them, and role playing go further in helping people change their thinking. Class study should be 80 percent real practice and 20 percent content delivery.

Most salespeople have succeeded on the basis of their intuitiveness and perceptiveness. VCS requires more in terms of logic, use of facts and data, and sharp analytics. This can be very intimidating and create a fear of failure, which itself can be barrier to learning. Even changes in terminology can be disconcerting, as in the paper industry, which tends to use "tons" instead of "revenue," or banking, which refers to "assets" rather than "revenue."

Assurances that these concepts are not difficult to master may allay some worries, but in the end it is the actual mastery of the content that builds confidence.

People need support and guidance as they make these sometimes difficult shifts. When Unifi set out to implement its profit growth initiative, which is its name for value creation selling, the sales force was intimidated. "At first it was a struggle just to get salespeople to talk to us in training sessions," recalls Ben Holder, Unifi's CIO and the executive who headed the transition training. "They were terribly nervous. In the first few days some of them couldn't even speak without their voice trembling. It was very unnerving sitting before the entire executive group and talking about your customer portfolio and book of business."

To break down the fear and reassure the salespeople, Holder asked them first to do a basic profile of their favorite customer using simple, easily obtained information and then present it to the senior executives and salespeople in the training session. "That's when things really began happening," Holder says. "When someone made his presentation you could see a blueprint emerge of the guy's ability. Without realizing it, he's telling you how he thinks, how he sees the customer, even how he sees the world.

"Getting financial information about each customer was one of the most difficult things for the salespeople, but we never ran into a situation where we couldn't get the information. In some cases, it was as simple as asking. Sometimes we had to check the credit agencies and sometimes we checked with other companies. It was helpful, too, just to know what kind of machines they had in their shop. That told us a lot about how much and what kind of materials they were buying from our competitors. It tells us what they can produce and we know the cost of the garment or product they make and we can multiply that by the capacity of the machine."

While gathering the right information was an initial challenge, the biggest change of mind-set came in doing the analysis of the customer's business, Holder says.

"They had to use finance and data analytics to build a business plan [a VAP in the parlance of value creation selling]. The sales force had worked off gut feel for so long that the whole concept of putting data onto that gut feeling was alien. We created a context for them by showing them that we play in a certain market and that our customers play in other markets but that they're two different worlds running in parallel. We had to get them to understand the world in which we operate, in which we have competitors, and we had to quantify the nature of those competitors with hard data. It was no longer acceptable to talk about your customer without talking about your customer's customers. What we wanted in the end was for them to be able to look at their business plan and explain to us what the competition in a given market is, what the obstacles are, who they need help from within the business, and what the market response may be."

The training sessions brought together a broad array of Unifi's executive corps with the sales force. Brian Parke, the Unifi CEO, attended every training session and made it clear to his other executives that if the training was his most important priority, then it should be theirs, too.

"The effect on the rest of the company was amazing," says Holder. "Managers in other functions started to make things happen because they knew at the morning meetings that somebody was going to point a finger at them if they didn't. It made the salespeople really feel better because now they had an enhanced stature within the company and could count on getting the type of support they needed to service their customers."

The meetings and the cooperation they fostered across silos within Unifi has resulted in what I call a social network. Here's Ben Holder again: "Now we have a system where people in operations, in everything other than sales, are connected to the sales effort because they know it's important to grow the business, take market share and support prices. Now everyone is sitting around talking about how we can sell more. We're still a way from having the perfect social network—there's still breakdowns in the process that prevent us from servicing a customer at the level we should—but more and more people know how important execution is. The more hearts and minds you win over, the faster the momentum builds."

What to Teach

The content for teaching value creation selling will evolve over time as instructors learn which techniques, examples, and exercises are most effective and as the abilities of the participants develop. Over time as VAPs are formulated and presented to customers there will be a pipeline of real-life examples that have not yet been accepted by the customer. They should form an important part of classroom exercises. In any case, everyone should come away from the training course with the following knowledge and skills:

- **What information they need from the customer, and how to get it, to create a VAP.** In the early stages of transitioning to value creation selling, the training sessions will include discussions and decisions about the structure and format of a VAP. It is likely that every company will need to create a unique format. A key skill then is how to ask the right questions of the right people in a way that provides the required information while building a foundation of trust. Training should include techniques for gaining access to people in the customer's shop other than the usual gatekeepers. Classroom discussions could revolve around which information is most useful and why, what the hurdles are to gathering it, how to overcome them, and best practices for keeping customer information up to date.

- **How to prepare a VAP from seemingly unconnected information from the customer and others.** It must be clear that the process of gathering information and shaping a value proposition is iterative. It requires multiple calls and visits to the customer, as well as pursuing other sources of information, and meeting with colleagues to flesh out details and discover the nuances that will point to a value-creating value proposition unique to each customer.

- **How to collaborate with and foster collaboration among various people in your own company.** Remember that VCS is a team sport. Sales leaders should learn how to include others in assessing information about the customer and identifying how their company can address the customer's needs and priorities. It is this collaboration that taps your organization's capabilities and best thinking and provides the foundation for a broader, deeper relationship with the customer. The quality of the dialogue has a huge impact on the quality of the value propositions you create. People can be trained in specific skills and techniques to facilitate dialogue among people with diverse points of view.

- **The language of business.** It is impossible to properly price your offering and convert it into business benefits without understanding your customer's total business. Sales leaders must be able to use the information in the VAP and the expertise of their colleagues to devise a coherent value proposition that is based on a crystal-clear view of the customer's physical needs. They must also be able to identify the quantitative and qualitative benefits of the value proposition and state it in the customer's language. That value proposition must be unique and differentiated, while at the same time producing a reasonable margin for the selling company.

- **The ability to foster an atmosphere of trust between the customer and the seller's own company.** People must know how important it is to develop a social network that binds the company and the customer long past the sale. The sales leader must learn to see the relationship as ongoing. The initial presentation of a value-creating proposition, for instance, is just the first step in the iterative process of gathering and incorporating information to sharpen and refine the value proposition.

- **The concept of TVO.** Salespeople need to master ways to express not just the cost reduction in the customer's shop, but also the benefits that accrue to the customer in terms of revenue growth and margin improvement. In addition they should be able to quantify, when appropriate, the gains in brand equity, market share, and cash generation. This is a critical area of training and each person needs to be tested at the end of the session to ensure that he or she has mastered the material. Those who score poorly in the test should receive additional instruction until they can demonstrate proficiency. In my observation, those who succeed in this area will have a very high probability of business success. They will be able to create winning value propositions.

Make Training Come Alive

Learning VCS requires repetitive practice with hands-on exercises in which the data is incomplete, messy, and sometimes confusing—just like the real world. As Unifi's experience demonstrates, the training process has to be highly interactive. Material that would ordinarily be presented as a lecture should be provided in writing for the class to read ahead of time. Class time itself should be reserved for discussing the ideas in the written material and ways to apply them to different situations. Extended question-and-answer periods will give instructors time to discern where people's understanding is getting blocked and what the participants' psychological hangups might be.

Most salespeople and most people working in functions other than accounting and finance do not know how to dissect a balance sheet or profit-and-loss statement. They also may not be familiar with the concepts and terminology of other aspects of the customers' businesses, such as marketing, operations, and research and development. And they won't be skilled at analyzing markets, competitive conditions, and industry trends. But those areas are all teachable in exercises in which instructors take the trainees through real-life situations involving actual customers. Participants in the training course can work on computer terminals and in small cross-functional groups to learn how to extract the necessary information from documents and databases, see where gaps exist, and understand how to complete a VAP.

As part of a cross-functional team, participants can instruct one another in their various specialties, creating bonds that will be useful later when a sales team has to work together. Through practice they also get more comfortable dealing with ambiguity and doing multiple iterations of the customer information and value proposition.

Instructors should oversee those cross-functional exercises, both to monitor whether the learning is taking hold and to watch for participants who are either too assertive for effective team play or too reserved to make a useful contribution. Some time should be set aside for individual tutorials, one-on-one coaching, and questions a participant might be embarrassed to raise in a group.

For the most part instructors should be the company's own executives. I believe the best training will come from the company's senior leaders, particularly the CEO and CFO. Not only can they explain the essential concept—how the customer makes money—but they can also evaluate the sales force, looking for strengths that can be built on and probing for weaknesses that must be fixed. But lower-ranking executives can also be effective instructors. They will share a common ground with and already know the salespeople and functional representatives. They can explain concepts using anecdotes and analogies drawn from a common experience, and they will be more easily available to the trainees who have questions or are seeking individual tutorials. That core instructional staff can be supplemented with invited guests. These might include executives from customers' organizations or people who have particular expertise or best practices to share. Academics or consultants can be brought in to teach highly specialized subjects.

Visits by executives from the customer's shop or by salespeople from other organizations where value creation selling is already being used are particularly valuable in training. Wall Street firms, for instance, already use value creation selling, whether or not they call it that. Each guest session should be scheduled for at least 90 minutes, with 20 minutes for the guest to describe his or her role or experience and the remaining 70 minutes devoted to questions from the trainees. When inviting executives from a customer's organization, it is especially useful to have two people attend: one who is someone the salespeople see or interact with regularly and another who represents a function that salespeople often do not see, such as finance or operations. Executives in the second category can be extremely helpful in explaining how to convert a physical value proposition into the customer's business language.

Training Through Apprenticeship

We all learned from our own school experience that once the classroom sessions end and we graduate, the real work begins. Implementing value creation selling is no different. Much can be learned in the classroom and practiced under the watchful eye of an instructor, but in the end only real-world experience will test and improve people's skills. This is truly learning by doing, which is why I call it an apprenticeship. There will be frustrations, questions, and disappointments as sales leaders and their functional team members begin to apply VCS to their everyday work.

An apprentice generally works under a skilled craftsman. In value creation selling the skilled people with the most knowledge about how to convert a company's offerings into a value proposition are the CEO and the CFO or business unit managers who have P & L responsibility. They have the breadth of experience and the deep understanding of the company's cost structure and technical abilities that permits them to come to the right conclusions about what the company can offer to a customer, and at what price. The apprenticeship system works best with regular focused practice. In one company the CEO and CFO achieved extremely good results by selecting five teams of five salespeople each. They conferred with a different team each day for 90 minutes to discuss the value propositions the salespeople were developing, offering ideas and comments to guide the formulation of the propositions. In five weeks—that is, five meetings with each team—the CEO and CFO found that not only were the salespeople becoming more adept at coming up with ways to create value, they were also working together as a social network to help one another. During the five weeks of apprenticeship the senior executives could see who got it, who could get it, and who simply couldn't adapt.

Not every CEO and CFO can devote that much time to the training effort. Making themselves available to the sales leaders and teams from time to time to give advice and counsel is, however, a huge opportunity to make the company customer centric. The CEO and CFO can offer advice in formal meetings when their schedule permits, or in telephone conference calls.

Communicating Successes

If you've trained the right salespeople and chosen the right customers to start with, you will likely have some early successes. It's important to let people know about them. Success begets success by raising morale and persuading skeptics that the new approach really will work. Most companies can turn to their corporate relations departments to create the necessary vehicles for communicating success, but I recommend some special tools that can be very effective.

A corporatewide webcast that tells the story of how a sales team approached a customer to extract information and design a value proposition is both entertaining and informative. A section of the corporate website can also be used for a weekly posting of tips and techniques that the sales teams have picked up. Or try holding a quarterly or semiannual value creation selling fair that uses exhibits to tell the success stories of various sales teams. And, of course, it's always beneficial to see success rewarded by promotions, pay, and other forms of recognition.

Measuring Progress

You have to realize that implementing value creation selling is a lengthy, arduous, and expensive undertaking with obstacles along the way. Reorienting the sales force is likely to be the first and biggest obstacle. A conscientious effort to foresee problems and correct them before they spin out of control will ease the path considerably.

The first and likely the largest problem will be ensuring that the sales force has the ability to convert the physical value proposition into quantified benefits stated in the customers' language. Value creation selling has a longer cycle time than the traditional approach to sales. That cycle time means salespeople don't get to practice their financial and analytical skills very often. The remedy is frequent testing and training aimed at identifying and fixing weaknesses in those skills.

A second common problem is that most salespeople have been functioning as solo operators. Under value creation selling they will be thrust into a much more collaborative role as leaders of their sales teams. They may find it uncomfortable and disconcerting to be responsible for gaining the cooperation of other functions without having direct hierarchical authority over them.

Of equal concern is that the salesperson who functioned best as a solo operator will lack the skills to analyze the customer's organization, pinpoint the locus of decision making, and reach the right people in the customer's power structure. A common fallacy among sales team leaders is that the "right people" means the top-most executive the salesperson can reach, rather than the decision maker or decision influencer, who may be relatively low in the customer's hierarchy.

Finally, some salespeople may be effective in obtaining information from and about the customer, but they may not be able to translate that intelligence into useful terms within their own organization. Focused training for those individuals can help them articulate information more clearly to the sales team.

Over time your training programs will become more formalized. At that point you can implement a certification program for the sales force that includes a formal test at the end of training to ensure that each person understands the concepts and methods of value creation selling.

Traditional sales organizations use only a few simple tools to measure how well their sales force is performing. Measuring the success of a VCS sales force is a more complex undertaking, but there are numerous ways to measure how well the sales force is adapting to VCS.

Because value creation selling emphasizes the creation of social organizations within the selling company and between the seller and the customer, you need instruments that measure how well those social organizations are operating. Feedback from customers through surveys and interviews is critical in assessing sales teams and their leaders. The sales force itself needs to understand the causes of both successes and failures. A success ratio can spark discussions within the sales force about why they won or lost, with particular emphasis on the failure to get an order when their price was the lowest and success when it was not. Another, more subtle tool would measure a salesperson's ability to diagnose the customer's decision-making processes and identify the decision makers, or the depth of interaction between your company and the customer's. Survey questions could also probe the extent of interaction between your sales force and the front end of the customer's company to gauge whether salespeople are learning about the customer's customer.

It is equally important to measure the internal processes that are vital to value creation selling. You should measure how well information and intelligence are being transferred within your company, and the sales team's knowledge of product and service offerings. Measuring the amount of face time the sales force has with customers will show the efficiency of sales support. Periodic self-evaluations by the sales force also provide insight into their skill and comfort levels in creating value propositions that get a premium price.

Following are some suggested metrics and mechanisms for tracking the progress and success of a VCS strategy. Measures done through surveys should be simple and not require the creation of a bureaucracy. They can be brief because they will be administered as often as every quarter, but at the same time they must be designed to plot progress.

- **Share of the customer's wallet.** This is without doubt the single best metric for measuring success, even though it is sometimes hard to obtain and often suffers from a time lag. Increased revenue is a key statistics, but so is improved margin, which will show whether you are able to get premium pricing.

- **Customer benefits.** This is a clear delineation in specific terms, for each account, of how the customer realizes the benefits promised.

- **Customer trust.** This survey, done in the customer's shop, measures on a scale of 1 to 10 the degree of trust the customer's executives have for the sales leader and team serving the account.

- **Customer-initiated contact.** This measures how frequently the customer initiates a request to the sales leader and team for advice about existing or future opportunities.

- **Internal collaboration.** This survey of sales leaders seeks their evaluation on a scale of 1 to 10 of how various functional silos are collaborating for a given customer.

- **Sales force certification.** This is a simple measure of what percentage of the sales force has received the required training and been certified.

- **Idea generation.** This survey of various functional areas seeks to measure the number of ideas fed to the functions by the sales team for future development (for example, product development, service development, changes in pricing approach, productivity improvements, or technology development).

- **Customer perception.** This survey asks the customer to evaluate on a scale of 1 to 10 how well the sales team really understands the customer's business, including the decision process and priorities.

Recruiting

As you expand your training to include more of the sales force, obviously not all of them will be able to make the grade. There will be instances in which enthusiasm exceeds ability and trainees must be placed elsewhere. Along the way, others will be promoted within the company or lured away by other companies. That naturally raises the question of where a company can find the necessary talent to replenish its VCS force.

The problem is not as vexing as it might seem. Supply always rises to meet demand. There are plenty of people in undergraduate business schools who have done some selling in the past. My advice in seeking entry-level salespeople is to visit universities in search of sales-oriented people with some business acumen. Test them to find those who have the right personality traits with reasonably good skills in business and financial analysis. Bring them in, train them, and look for leadership skills that will enable them to become sales executives. In high-value selling that involves multimillion-dollar sales, it might be necessary to seek out MBA students who have the business acumen, the personality for selling, the knowledge to extract information, and the skills in group dynamics. Consulting firms can be a source of more experienced and skilled salespeople, but recruiting them requires some caution. If people don't have the gregarious personality and psychology that lets them work in groups and build relationships, they won't succeed.

Bringing Independent Sales Representatives Along

When your sales force works directly for you, you can reshape it by providing formal training and changing the hiring criteria and incentives. But many smaller companies use self-employed sales reps. The key to winning their cooperation lies in—you guessed it—helping create value for their business. The trick is to do what Tim Ahern did. He used value creation selling to provide solutions for his independent sales reps so that they, in turn, could provide solutions for their customers.

Ahern bought BCI Burke Company, a manufacturer of playground equipment for schools and municipalities, in 1997 when the founding family decided to sell the business. Ahern's previous experience was with big companies that deployed large sales forces. He was shocked at first to discover how different it was to be selling through independent sales representatives.

"Most of the rep firms were small businesses of one to six people. Typically, the owner was the chief cook and bottle washer. They were usually undercapitalized and didn't have a business plan. They were short-staffed and didn't have enough salespeople. But what really surprised me is that I thought everyone would want to improve, to grow their business. Now I know better. When I go in and talk to the principle of a rep firm, I want to know how they think, what vision they have for their future. I need to determine if their outlook is in line with Burke's. If it is, we can work together to grow their business and ours. If it isn't, we've got to look elsewhere."

Ahern found the kind of sales rep he wanted in Jay Robertson, a former playground construction manager in Dallas, Texas, who had taken on the Burke playground line just before Ahern bought the company. Robertson said the Burke line of equipment was high-quality but that the family owners clearly were more interested in selling the company than building it. With only several months of experience selling Burke equipment, Robertson was apprehensive when Ahern bought the company.

"I was worried because I was the low guy on the totem pole, but it didn't take long to see that Tim was really interested in building the business, not just his business, but the rep business, too," Robertson says. "It was very rare to see a manufacturer who truly cares about the people who sell his product."

Ahern recalls that his favorable impression of Jay and his wife, who together run Child's Play in Dallas, grew over time.

"In the first year Jay and Kathy were struggling, having a hard time making the payments to Burke on product that they had out," he says. "But they kept us up to speed, did what we asked, and if there was an issue they brought it to us. We didn't have to call them—they called us. Right there, I knew we had someone interested in his own business who also respected my business."

Ahern went to Dallas to spend some time with the Robertsons to see if he could help them improve their rep operation. After driving around Dallas with Robertson in his pickup truck, Tim saw two things: Robertson was a born salesman, and he was spending far too much time overseeing the construction and installation of the playground equipment he sold.

"What's preventing you from doing more selling?" Ahern asked.

"I have to spend all my time making sure the installations are done right," Robertson said.

Ahern, using a classic value creation selling approach, kept asking Robertson questions about his interests, how he managed his time, what he wanted his firm to become, until Robertson saw the solution to his problem: find someone else to oversee installations so that he could spend more time selling.

"What changed when Tim took over Burke is that it forced me to have a clear business focus, something I had never had before. I was impressed that Tim would come down and take the time to talk about things, not just bang on us to get more sales. I never looked at my business from the outside in. I just went day to day, trying to get things done. Tim gave me a long-term goal and a plan to reach it. He helped me see what was important, what I was doing wrong that I could fix and what I was doing right that I could do more of."

Ahern downplays his role in the transformation of Child's Play. "All I needed to do was just water the plant, then get out of the way," he says. "Since 1997 Jay has grown a thousand percent in sales volume in a pre-dominantly flat industry. We're a relatively humble and small business, but when you see that kind of growth pattern, you know you've got a rep who knows what he's doing."

Now Ahern and Robertson work closely to be sure that Burke and Child's Play are offering customers a value proposition that's worth a premium payment. The proposition starts with on-time delivery of quality products that are installed correctly and then warranted for the life of the playground. Replacement of broken parts covered under warranty is done free of material and labor charges. As a result Burke is able to charge double-digit premiums against competing playground equipment manufacturers.

"For commercial playground equipment a large part of the customer's total cost of ownership is maintenance and replacement over the life of the product," Ahern explains. "A lot of municipalities and schools don't fully understand that, and when you show them the related costs and tell them you're going to cover it, they don't always believe you. A big part of the rep's job is making sure that the potential customer understands the value proposition we're offering and what it will mean to them financially over the life of the product. I know that in this business if they go with somebody else, we haven't explained it well enough. When we lose a sale I feel that the customer has made a serious mistake."

The creation of an effective sales force demands tenacity for selecting the right people and training them. The training involves an experiential format and repetitive exercises. Top management must participate and demonstrate sincere commitment to the process. The lack of effective training will be self-defeating in the execution of the transformation. The value of this training becomes highly visible when the sales leader and his or her team make the presentation to the customer. The how of that presentation is described in Chapter 6.

6

Making the Sale

Six months after Sturgis introduced its new approach to selling, Charlie was a new man. He passed the certification to do value creation selling and was talking to customers with renewed interest. He found that some of his long-time friends in purchasing knew far more about their companies than he'd realized; what they didn't know they were often willing to find out. Charlie was asking them different kinds of questions and getting greater insight into their businesses. He was also doing his own research, and though he was still shaky when it came to the financial information, he was getting better at sorting through it.

For the past several months, he had doggedly chased a new account and assembled a team of colleagues from various departments at Sturgis who were equally enthusiastic about value creation selling. They had helped gather information, some of them venturing to contact people in the customer's shop for the first time ever. The sales team had met several times to analyze all the material they'd collected, and they'd pinpointed the customer's concern about top-line growth. The customer was expected to deliver close to double-digit gains in sales under intense competitive pressure. Charlie's team had brainstormed ways Sturgis could help the customer boost sales, in part by touting the technical superiority of its products using data the Sturgis team assembled, and they'd crafted a value proposition based on Sturgis's ability to help the customer advance technologically.

Now it was time to present that proposition to the customer. It wasn't just a matter of driving over to the customer's headquarters and making a PowerPoint presentation. Indeed, the team would all attend, and they wouldn't use PowerPoint at all. Instead, Charlie would make an introductory presentation, and then each team member would describe the portion of the proposition that fell under his or her department at Sturgis. Then Charlie would wind it up with a short but detailed explanation of the benefits the customer would realize, both physical and financial, with emphasis on meeting revenue growth expectations. The CFO was prepared to detail how those benefits would affect the customer's income statement and balance sheet.

The team had rehearsed their presentations until they knew them by heart. They had also considered what questions the customer's people might have, what objections they might raise and what changes they might want to make in the value proposition. Sturgis was prepared to make them, and the team would not be disheartened if they left the room without agreement on a deal. They knew they were on the right track.

By the time the team is ready to make the presentation, n members should have at least a passing familiarity all or most of the customer's people who will attend presentation. It is here that the nitty-gritty work of eloping the VAP can help. If the preparation of the P has been thorough, it will pinpoint the decision ker. But if that information is lacking, and it often is in first attempts to create a VAP, the team at the very t should make their best guess about who among the omer's people are the decision makers, who are the uencers, and whether the influencers will likely favor ppose the value proposition. By trying to anticipate uments against the value proposition, the team can k about ways to overcome those objections. The abil- o mention a few facts and data points can go a long in countering objections based merely on an individ- s impressions and gut reactions.

Pitch: The Dynamics of Dialogue

big day finally arrives. Dress rehearsals are over. This e real thing. The formal presentation to the customer rhaps the most important milestone in the entire de- pment of the value creation proposition. It tests how d a job the sales leader has done in collecting the infor- ion that went into the VAP, how effectively the team worked together to craft the proposition, and how te the sales leader has been in making the right trade- among the various interests within his or her own pany and the customer's. The point is to establish that r company has the necessary expertise and a deep in-

After a sales team has used the VAP to craft what they believe to be the best response to a customer's needs and priorities, it's time to make the sales pitch. But presenting a *value creation proposition* to the customer is nothing like the typical sales call that most salespeople are accustomed to. In value creation selling much more work goes into preparation, in part because the sales call now involves a team of people whose presentations and responses to customer questions must be planned and coordinated. And because the sales call incorporates more background information and analysis, the value creation proposition itself is more complex than a simple "Here's my product, what price will you pay?" presentation. While the call must concisely convey the fact that you understand the customer's business and have a specific offering that provides a broad range of benefits, you have to allow that you might have missed something.

The call is above all an opportunity for further questioning and observation of the customer's organization. Rather than signing a contract at that first sales call, it is likely that the sales team will return to the office to figure out ways to modify the value proposition to more specifically address concerns that emerged during the discussion. Honing and perfecting the value proposition to meet the customer's needs is at the heart of value creation selling.

Preparing the Pitch

A lot of work goes into shaping a value proposition, and there's a tendency to want to let the customer know how

hard you've worked. But as you prepare the pitch, you have to resist that temptation. Instead of trying to wow the customer with the data you've amassed, let the value proposition speak for itself. The content of the value creation proposition itself will be sufficient to demonstrate the effort and thought the sales team has invested to help the customer meet his or her most important priorities. It is much better to avoid complexity and to keep the presentation short and to the point.

Typically the presentation will begin with the team leader making a clear statement of the challenge the seller's company is going to help the customer meet or the opportunity that it will help the customer seize, followed by an explanation of the physical benefits the value proposition will provide—shorter lead times, smaller inventories, or more productive sales calls, for example. Then members of the sales team can lay out specific details of the parts of the value proposition they are expert in.

Dennis Simon, CEO of XRoads Solutions Group, a professional services firm, has, along with his team, been making value creation sales pitches for several years. He finds it helpful in preparing the pitch to think in terms of themes. A broad or general theme—reducing inventory and financing costs, for example—could guide the initial and final parts of the presentation. Specific themes—identifying logistical bottlenecks, selecting the right vendors for fast turnaround, and the financial savings involved in lower inventories and reduced financing costs—provide the focus for the middle of the pitch. Individual team members take responsibility for developing and presenting the specific themes, mastering the facts and details behind them. Each of XRoad's team members also

prepares several short examples or anec[dotes] than a few minutes each to amplify and il[lustrate a spe]cific theme. Saying, for instance, "Wher[...] something similar for another company [...] offering more concrete and builds credib[ility...] the team members must also understand [how the] themes are interrelated.

The sales leader should develop som[e...] rules governing the sales call. Should team [members be al]lowed to interrupt one another's presen[tation? Which] team member will answer questions about [...] Can each team member decide on the spo[t whether to] modify the particular provisions of the va[lue proposition] that are his or her area of expertise?

So that each team member understands [his or her role] in the sales call, the pitch should be re[hearsed several] times. Colleagues who are not part of the [team can be in]vited in for some of these practice session[s...] critique the presentation with an eye towa[rd eliminating] complexity and ambiguity. These practic[e sessions] can be invaluable tools for generating que[stions the cus]tomer might ask and for sharing knowle[dge about how] each team member will work with the cust[omer's organi]zation during the actual sales call. It's also [a good time to] review competitors' potential offerings a[nd to assess] their strong and weak points, particularly i[n terms of the] specific customer problems that the value c[reation propo]sition will solve. The team can decide du[ring these ses]sions how far to go in making adjustment[s to the value] proposition: what changes can be made du[ring the sales] call, which ones should be worked out late[r...] and who should make that judgment call o[n...]

terest in solving the customer's problems or helping him
seize an opportunity.

"Our presentation is almost an 'overwhelming force'
concept," says Clayton LiaBraaten of INFONXX. "A
salesperson may lead the team presentation, but the presenting team is heavy with operational and technical expertise. We don't want to outnumber or outmuscle the
prospect, but we want our business capabilities fully repre-
sented," he explains. "That allows us to establish ourselves
as the subject matter experts, and we have a better chance of
winning the confidence of the operations, finance, and technology folks in the prospect audience. If we can establish
ourselves as thought leaders, we can leverage that leadership to draw more information out of them. There's usually at least one guy in the room who sees the value in what
we're presenting and says, 'There's no harm in sharing information.' That's when the dialogue really opens up."

It is important to understand, however, that the formal
presentation is not necessarily the day of reckoning. While
you may leave the meeting with an agreement, it is just as
likely that you will leave without one. But even then you
will certainly have a better understanding of how your
team can modify the value creation proposition to make it
more attractive to the customer.

The quantified benefits that are an integral part of the
value proposition require that at least one member of
the sales team be grounded in finance. If the customer
brings the CFO or a financial analyst to the pitch, try to
seat your own finance person close by. Their finance person will likely be the most conservative person in the
room. He or she will invariably be thinking about how
the company will finance the purchase, what it will do to

the value of the business, and how it will affect cash flow and borrowing. Seating your own finance expert across the table allows the two experts to talk face-to-face rather than down the length of a table. If they can develop a rapport, your finance person can call the customer's finance person to see if his or her concerns are threatening the proposal.

It's your choice how to present the value proposition, but don't assume it has to be a flashy PowerPoint presentation. Paper often works better. If you go that way, the basics of the value proposition should be laid out in a booklet distributed to everyone attending the pitch before the presentation begins. Each specific point of the proposition should be stated on a different page, with ample room for the reader to take notes. In any case, each team member's presentation should be succinct and to the point. Before beginning each presentation team members should be sure to invite interruptions and questions during the course of the presentation.

Given sufficient practice the actual presentation of the value creation proposition should go smoothly. The real work begins when the formal presentation ends. The dynamics of the dialogue will have revealed much about the customer's thinking and will suggest some appropriate responses. The key lesson is to listen, don't tell. The sales team, and especially the leader, should exercise critical listening skills. Who on the customer's side is asking what questions? What is the general thrust of their comments? Do they seem concerned about some aspect of their business you hadn't considered? If the customer's team is questioning specific details, that isn't a big problem. But if they're indicating that they don't share your ideas about what their biggest priorities are, you may have a serious flaw in your proposal. Can you discern from the questions and comments whether the customer is making different assumptions about the value proposition than your team had when you developed it? It is possible that during the research phase of the VAP you failed to discover something, or maybe the company's senior management is thinking about repositioning the business in a way that makes your value proposition less valuable. Is the decision maker focused on a specific aspect of the proposition, perhaps one that the team had not expected to be carefully scrutinized? Especially among large companies there is a concern that smaller suppliers do not have the depth of talent to deliver a solution if a key player on the supplier's team quits, becomes ill, or is hired away.

You should make note of those issues as the dialogue progresses, not only for future reference in honing the value proposition, but also to signal to the customer that the team is listening carefully and noting the customer's ideas and objections. A list of every objection raised during the presentation provides the framework for follow-up work that keeps your team in close contact with the customer. At appropriate points during the discussion, you should repeat the customer's statements to demonstrate that you are hearing and understanding what is being said. If you're answering a question, remember at the end of your answer to ask specifically, "Does that answer your question?" Differences in the tenor of the comments or questions among the people present can be evidence of internal differences in the customer's shop. These should be fished out.

When Dennis Simon of XRoads Solutions Group

detects significant differences of opinion among a customer's people, he often finds that he can defuse conflict by turning his presentation into a tutorial on the issue at hand, explaining both sides of the issue in order to give support to both sides of the disputing factions. "Sometimes the ultimate decision maker is the entire customer team," he explains. "They have to come together to decide if they want to look at the question objectively without a preconceived notion that something is right or wrong. We try to go in and create a decision-making environment for the customer where one might not have existed. That way we can satisfy each individual's personal and professional needs."

It isn't unusual for the dialogue to stall, drift off into irrelevant areas, or become circular. When that seems to be happening the sales team leader should step in to redirect the conversation into a useful channel. One valuable question to get the discussion back to joint problem solving is, "What are some alternatives that can solve your problem?" Or to help ferret out the deepest concerns among the customer's people you might ask, "What risks are you facing with regard to your own customers?"

Unspoken Questions

Although the customer may not articulate his or her deepest concerns, underlying the entire dialogue, three critical questions will be very much on the customer's mind:

- **Is the value proposition realistic?** Keep in mind that most customers approach a sales pitch with

After a sales team has used the VAP to craft what they believe to be the best response to a customer's needs and priorities, it's time to make the sales pitch. But presenting a *value creation proposition* to the customer is nothing like the typical sales call that most salespeople are accustomed to. In value creation selling much more work goes into preparation, in part because the sales call now involves a team of people whose presentations and responses to customer questions must be planned and coordinated. And because the sales call incorporates more background information and analysis, the value creation proposition itself is more complex than a simple "Here's my product, what price will you pay?" presentation. While the call must concisely convey the fact that you understand the customer's business and have a specific offering that provides a broad range of benefits, you have to allow that you might have missed something.

The call is above all an opportunity for further questioning and observation of the customer's organization. Rather than signing a contract at that first sales call, it is likely that the sales team will return to the office to figure out ways to modify the value proposition to more specifically address concerns that emerged during the discussion. Honing and perfecting the value proposition to meet the customer's needs is at the heart of value creation selling.

Preparing the Pitch

A lot of work goes into shaping a value proposition, and there's a tendency to want to let the customer know how hard you've worked. But as you prepare the pitch, you have to resist that temptation. Instead of trying to wow the customer with the data you've amassed, let the value proposition speak for itself. The content of the value creation proposition itself will be sufficient to demonstrate the effort and thought the sales team has invested to help the customer meet his or her most important priorities. It is much better to avoid complexity and to keep the presentation short and to the point.

Typically the presentation will begin with the team leader making a clear statement of the challenge the seller's company is going to help the customer meet or the opportunity that it will help the customer seize, followed by an explanation of the physical benefits the value proposition will provide—shorter lead times, smaller inventories, or more productive sales calls, for example. Then members of the sales team can lay out specific details of the parts of the value proposition they are expert in.

Dennis Simon, CEO of XRoads Solutions Group, a professional services firm, has, along with his team, been making value creation sales pitches for several years. He finds it helpful in preparing the pitch to think in terms of themes. A broad or general theme—reducing inventory and financing costs, for example—could guide the initial and final parts of the presentation. Specific themes—identifying logistical bottlenecks, selecting the right vendors for fast turnaround, and the financial savings involved in lower inventories and reduced financing costs—provide the focus for the middle of the pitch. Individual team members take responsibility for developing and presenting the specific themes, mastering the facts and details behind them. Each of XRoad's team members also prepares several short examples or anecdotes of no more than a few minutes each to amplify and illustrate the specific theme. Saying, for instance, "When we were doing something similar for another company . . ." makes the offering more concrete and builds credibility. Of course the team members must also understand how the various themes are interrelated.

The sales leader should develop some basic ground rules governing the sales call. Should team members be allowed to interrupt one another's presentations? Which team member will answer questions about specific topics? Can each team member decide on the spot if and how to modify the particular provisions of the value proposition that are his or her area of expertise?

So that each team member understands his or her role in the sales call, the pitch should be rehearsed several times. Colleagues who are not part of the team can be invited in for some of these practice sessions and asked to critique the presentation with an eye toward eliminating complexity and ambiguity. These practice presentations can be invaluable tools for generating questions the customer might ask and for sharing knowledge about how each team member will work with the customer's organization during the actual sales call. It's also a good time to review competitors' potential offerings and to identify their strong and weak points, particularly in regard to the specific customer problems that the value creation proposition will solve. The team can decide during these sessions how far to go in making adjustments to the value proposition: what changes can be made during the sales call, which ones should be worked out later at the office, and who should make that judgment call on the fly.

By the time the team is ready to make the presentation, team members should have at least a passing familiarity with all or most of the customer's people who will attend the presentation. It is here that the nitty-gritty work of developing the VAP can help. If the preparation of the VAP has been thorough, it will pinpoint the decision maker. But if that information is lacking, and it often is in the first attempts to create a VAP, the team at the very least should make their best guess about who among the customer's people are the decision makers, who are the influencers, and whether the influencers will likely favor or oppose the value proposition. By trying to anticipate arguments against the value proposition, the team can think about ways to overcome those objections. The ability to mention a few facts and data points can go a long way in countering objections based merely on an individual's impressions and gut reactions.

The Pitch: The Dynamics of Dialogue

The big day finally arrives. Dress rehearsals are over. This is the real thing. The formal presentation to the customer is perhaps the most important milestone in the entire development of the value creation proposition. It tests how good a job the sales leader has done in collecting the information that went into the VAP, how effectively the team has worked together to craft the proposition, and how astute the sales leader has been in making the right trade-offs among the various interests within his or her own company and the customer's. The point is to establish that your company has the necessary expertise and a deep in-

In value creation selling the price of delivering a value proposition is seldom a single number. Rather, because the proposition can be complex, discussions of price center on what I call *price architecture.* By that I mean the price could include variables such as incentive payments for better-than-promised performance, bonus payments for on-time delivery or special credit terms. The point is that both sides need to walk away from the agreement with a sense of satisfaction and feeling of accomplishment.

After the Pitch

Too often in traditional selling the sales pitch either succeeds or fails and the salesperson moves on to the next customer and the next pitch. In value creation selling the sales pitch is just another beginning, whether or not it succeeds. If the customer accepts your value proposition, perhaps with some modification, you have to be sure that it is not only delivered on time and as described, but that it fulfills the promises you made.

Chances are, however, that you'll leave the pitch meeting with a new list of objections, suggestions, and impressions. The first thing to do is let the customer know you heard her objections and suggestions. A letter, an e-mail, or a telephone call that reiterates the objections and enumerates the suggestions your team made during the presentation will reassure the customer that you're still very interested in her business and will do everything you can to refine your offering. This communication should also set a specific date and time to meet again. To address specific objections or suggestions, the appropriate team members should reach the appropriate people in the customer's organization for elaboration or to ask specific questions.

This is a good time to seek more access. You can try to meet with the person you've identified as the decision maker to clarify her objections, or you could ask to visit with people who could explain specific areas of the customer's business. You might even offer to sign a confidentiality agreement to put the customer at ease. When Dennis Simon of XRoads made a proposal that didn't quite resonate with the customer, he followed up with a request to explore the logistic problem the customer was experiencing in China. The customer agreed to let the consulting team in, and based on what they learned, the team was able to shape a value proposition that was exactly what the company needed to improve its cycle time, cost structure, and market position.

In following up with the customer, you can change the scope of the value proposition, narrowing or expanding it as appropriate and resetting the customer's expectations. You might, for example, suggest a shorter-term contract to a customer who is skeptical that you can deliver, or shape a value proposition focused more on efficiency than on revenue growth if you learn that cash is a major concern. In one case, a consulting firm knew that a potential client wanted to brand its commodity products globally and created a value proposition to help the client meet that priority. During the assignment the firm learned that the client company lacked some of the capabilities it needed to meet that objective. Based on those additional insights into the customer's organization, the consulting firm altered its value proposition, and in so doing helped the customer build a brand in a small region—something the firm knew would succeed. The firm then assembled the facts to show how the value proposition would be beneficial to the customer's business.

Subsequent pitches of the evolving value proposition take much the same form as the original pitch, but for obvious reasons they should be shorter and more focused on resolving specific objections or explaining the modifications made to the value proposition. Each reiteration of the value proposition should move the sales team and the customer closer to agreement while giving the sales team invaluable insight into the inner workings of the customer's decision-making process.

But not all sales pitches will end in success. If at the second or third sales meetings the customer is raising new objections or finding excuses for not reaching a final agreement, the sales team should begin to question the customer's sincerity. The unfortunate truth is that some customers are not worth keeping.

Lessons Learned and Continuing Dialogue

Once the sale is made and the delivery and implementation of the value proposition is taking place, your sales team should be working to identify the next opportunity to help the customer succeed. It may be something as simple as fine-tuning the solution you have already delivered or it could involve extending the value proposition you just sold to other products or regions or divisions. New opportunities will emerge as the sales team continues to

meet with their counterparts in the customer's shop in social or business settings. These meetings can and should
include conversations that have nothing to do with selling
your products or services. Instead, they should be used to
brainstorm new ideas for the customer, to discuss what is
changing in the external environment and what it means
to both your company, your customer, and your customer's customers. Everyone will benefit from exercising
these mental muscles. When appropriate these sessions
can be facilitated by the CEO of your company, who
might invite a diverse group of people from the customer's
shop to spend the day talking about what the future holds
for their business.

The sales pitch and its outcome will also provide the
sales team with valuable lessons that may need to be incorporated into value propositions other teams are preparing.
Those lessons need to be shared. The most effective means
for sharing is for top management to conduct a monthly
review of lessons learned, communicated broadly to managers and sales leaders via a webcast or company memo.
Conducted regularly and frequently, such sessions go far
in fostering a customer-centric mind-set throughout the
company.

7

Sustaining the Process

It was time for Jack Garrett, the CEO of Sturgis, to meet with his CFO to set next year's budget and contemplate the revenue target for the upcoming fiscal year. Jack was pleased with the progress they'd made in the ten months since they'd introduced value creation selling, although the top line hadn't moved much. Yet. He was confident their efforts would soon begin to pay off and then accelerate two and three years out. He didn't want to choke off the training needed to sustain the VCS initiative for the sake of cutting costs, despite the fact that the big gains in sales would take some time to materialize. As VCS took hold, Sturgis would be able to sell more, and at premium prices, and revenue would take an upward turn. Sturgis had failed to meet revenue expectations for the past two years and investors were getting wary, but Jack and the CFO agreed they had a credible story to tell and evidence to back it up.

Transformation of the sales force and sales management was well underway. Other functions such as

finance and manufacturing were beginning to collaborate with the sales force. The company was making
headway in a number of new accounts, and margins on
new business were improving. Even headhunters had
noticed the change: they'd tried to snatch two of Sturgis's newly trained, best salespeople.

To sustain the commitment to VCS and embed it in
the organization, Jack was changing the reward structure, charging leaders with responsibility to coach their
people on business acumen, and sitting in on reviews
to be sure the change process didn't inadvertently get
undermined by short-term pressures. He was also
working with his CFO and COO to decide how best
to monitor progress. The change was not complete, but
Sturgis was gaining momentum, and almost everyone
who did business with Sturgis knew it.

Unless top management makes value creation selling its
top priority the process will simply become another fad of
the day. Top management must integrate the value creation selling initiative into virtually all management decisions: the selection and promotion of people, the choice of
businesses, the targeting of market segments and customers, resource allocation, operating reviews, and budget
preparation. Senior management must have the energy
and tenacity to drive the change.

Are we helping our customers prosper and sharing in
their prosperity? This is the central question that should
always be on people's minds, and the organization must
function in a way that delivers an affirmative answer.

Some leaders may decide to change the organizational structure, but what matters most is how people work together. The company's social system must ensure that the relevant departments and people synchronize with one another. Without that all-encompassing change in how people work—who they exchange information with, what they spend their energy on, how they determine their priorities—value creation selling will not take root.

VCS also requires a major shift in people's mental orientation, from focusing solely on cost reduction to also thinking about revenue growth. This shift puts some leaders on uncomfortable ground, because efforts to increase revenue are inherently less certain than moves to boost productivity and reduce costs. The shift must be evident in the company's reward system and budgeting processes. Leaders have many chances to reinforce it in operating, budget, and performance reviews.

Tackle Value Creation Selling from the Top Down

Because sales will bear the brunt of the changes that occur in the transition to value creation selling, it is critical that the entire sales management team be willing and able to lead the change. Almost right away the CEO should assess whether senior-level sales managers, especially the executive vice president of sales, have the skills to lead VCS—the ability to lead sales teams and engage peers in other silos, as well as all the skills VCS itself entails. They must also be equipped to lead the change. Top leaders, including the head of sales, will be asked to "lead by doing," so they will have to master the skills and tools for VCS. They should go through the same training and certification process that their salespeople will be required to pass. Even the head of sales must be willing and able to put herself in the role of selling something through the value creation selling process.

Some executives at this level will be unwilling to abandon the comfort of their plush offices and get their hands dirty by actually creating a VAP. But unless they can do it, they won't truly understand how value creation selling works and thus will not be able to create an effective sales force. If the executive vice president of sales doesn't "get it," then the CEO has to get someone else for that position. That is true of the senior sales executive in a business unit as well. You might worry that taking out a sales manager puts customer relationships at risk and hurts sales force morale, but that has not been the case among companies that have undertaken value creation selling.

Once you know you have the right sales leaders at the top, you should drill deeper. How good are the top sales executives in each of your lines of business? Do they understand the need for the change, what it is intended to accomplish, and how? What is their "genetic code," or set of common traits? What is their current dominant psychology? What do they think is critical in their current jobs? At bottom, you want to determine if they are willing and able to lead VCS. At a minimum, sales managers will need excellent communication skills. They will have to be good at developing the company's social system and knitting it with the customer's. They must be effective in a collaborative environment. One individual cannot be allowed to impede the organization's progress.

The structure of the sales department should be evaluated as well. How many layers of sales management does the company have? Typically there are three levels: executive vice president, regional vice president, and district sales managers. You should rethink the expertise needed at each level and the way those leaders should be spending their time. They should all be certified in VCS, for instance, and they should be personally involved in training their sales force for VCS and spend considerable time on it. It is not unusual to find that the top two layers of the sales organization spend no time on training salespeople or even district sales managers. Instead, they contract out the teaching. But value creation selling requires sales managers' constant hands-on attention. Outside trainers may be useful in supplemental roles, but they cannot ensure VCS gets properly ingrained.

Beyond mastering VCS and helping others learn it, leaders of the sales organization should spend their time on other activities to support VCS, such as developing mechanisms for salespeople to share best practices and learn from one another. They will also have to sort out who can and cannot make the grade in value creation selling. As some salespeople are removed, sales leaders will have to recruit new hires to replace them and be sure the new recruits are thoroughly trained. They will also have a role to play in changing the reward system and in linking the sales force with other functions and departments to ensure sales gets the support it needs.

Build Organizational Support

Value creation selling is team selling. The sales force cannot do its job unless the rest of the organization provides the quality, skill mix, and responsiveness to support their efforts. Senior leaders must create linkages between the various functions of the business.

One of the biggest challenges facing the sales force is to build credibility among colleagues in other silos. In the past, salespeople have made promises to customers and thrown the problem "over the wall" for others to deliver. Operations, finance, and legal have their own priorities and pace and aren't necessarily responsive to the sales department's requests. Pricing is a common source of friction between finance and sales. Some sales leaders feel the finance department is too slow to concur on pricing decisions and is unresponsive to customers' needs. In value creation selling, salespeople cannot be ignored. They are now team leaders directing the work of lawyers, financial experts, and others. Senior leaders have to keep a close eye on how these relationships are changing. Monthly surveys that ask the sales force how well other departments are collaborating can identify areas and departments that need attention. The value account plan is the focal point for creating linkages, but leaders should look for other ways to change attitudes, such as training and leading by example.

Each silo within the organization must reconsider its role with an eye toward identifying and eliminating bottlenecks to the formulation and delivery of a value proposition. The legal department, for example, might focus on eliminating delays in contracts, perhaps by simplifying contract language or by meeting directly with the customer's legal department to reach agreements on some terms before the solution is presented. The finance department can teach the sales force how to do financial analysis and cost-benefit analysis and how to use other analytical tools to learn more about the customer. Finance representatives might visit their counterparts at the customer's company to establish a method of continuous credit review so that terms can be reached quickly when a solution is presented.

The marketing department has a critical role to play through upstream marketing, that is, determining with granularity who the best customers are and exactly what products and services the company can create that will solve those customers' specific needs. A big part of that job is figuring out who you want to sell to and what they really need. It isn't as easy as it sounds, but it is fundamental to effective downstream marketing, that is, advertising, brand building, and public relations.

It would be useful for the marketing department to map out its overall market and its different segments. Such a map has several uses. First, it can be used to compare one market segment against another to see where possible relationships might exist between segments. Second, it can provide the analytical framework to determine which customers will be willing to pay a premium price for helping differentiate themselves from competitors. Finally, it can help the company identify the major competitors in each market segment and analyze their positioning and marketing strategies to find ways to win more business away from them.

Sales support in value creation selling extends beyond the normal definition to include such things as special studies of the customer's customers. If there are ten attributes to your customer's product or service, which one or two dominate the buying decision?

Focus on Both Revenue and Cost

Most senior managers know with certainty that if they boost productivity while maintaining revenues, they'll reduce costs and increase profits. Cost reduction is familiar ground and involves little risk. But there is a limit to how far cost reduction can go before it begins to impinge on the company's ability to innovate and grow. Value creation selling will help you increase revenues, but it may require you to spend some more money to achieve that growth. The question is, how much are you likely to boost your revenues by incurring those costs? What is your *revenue productivity*?

Take a company that has ten salespeople. Two of its salespeople are stars who bring in a lot of revenue and are paid $250,000 a year. Six salespeople are good at their jobs but don't produce nearly as much revenue as the stars; they are paid $150,000 a year. The last two salespeople haven't kept up with the changing market and don't produce much revenue, so they are paid $80,000. What if the two worst employees were replaced by two more stars? Payroll costs would rise, of course, but gains in revenue year after year would make the extra costs worthwhile. Viewed that way, the higher salary costs aren't so much a cost as an investment. There are risks involved—how do you know you're hiring superstars who can produce the necessary revenue to make their salaries worthwhile?— but accepting those risks may be the only way for you to increase your revenues.

It can be expensive to undertake value creation selling. Before trying to adopt it, you should analyze your businesses and markets to determine where it makes sense to invest the time, money, and attention required. Some unprofitable or low-profit businesses can achieve remarkable gains through value creation selling. But applying VCS to businesses in moribund markets or with minuscule market share compared to their much larger competitors may not amount to much. Selecting the right markets is crucial to minimizing your risks and improving your likelihood of success. It will boost your revenue productivity.

In some cases you may have to redefine markets. Not all customers are good customers. Sophisticated and open-minded customers will see the value of entering into a closer relationship with a seller; that's where you should concentrate your VCS efforts. But there will also be customers who are suspicious or simply not interested in joining the process. You can still sell them products. In fact, companies that have undertaken value creation selling report that even after several years, about 30 percent of their revenue comes from purely transactional sales. You can pursue businesses that don't lend themselves to VCS through other approaches such as a Web-based strategy.

Decisions about where you apply a VCS approach will drive your decisions about resource allocation and may well reshape your company's business portfolio. In many companies the CEO encourages business units to devote their efforts to hitting home runs, the big breakthroughs that produce huge gains in sales. Such breakthroughs, while legitimate goals, occur only occasionally. Sustained profitable revenue growth comes through numerous singles and doubles that produce incremental gains. Those incremental gains often build upon one another. While value creation selling allows for home runs, its focus is on sustained incremental gains. It becomes the CEO's goal to establish a culture of calculated risk taking that encourages the sales teams to explore possibilities that would never have been possible under the traditional sales orientation.

Even decisions about how to organize the sales force should be based on revenue productivity. In most cases it is less expensive to build a sales force around geographical territories. Salespeople in a given territory handle the company's entire product line for a diverse array of customers. But as business becomes more complex it becomes increasingly difficult for a salesperson to understand all the products she is selling and to know the companies and industries well. A sales force organized by industry segments, on the other hand, is typically more expensive, but each salesperson can focus on fewer products and develop closer, more knowledgeable relationships with her customers. With deeper knowledge of the customer's industry, she can do a better job of shaping value propositions.

Put Revenue at the Center of Budgeting

The budgeting process is where the focus on revenue becomes real, where it gets communicated and implemented. That's when people get together to decide who is accountable for what. It provides the discipline for measuring performance against quantifiable milestones, usually monthly or quarterly. But just as traditional selling is nothing like value creation selling, traditional budgeting is nothing like the budgeting you should do when you adopt value creation selling.

The budgets of most companies devote dozens or even hundreds of lines to various cost categories, reflecting management's fixation on costs. Only a few lines are devoted to sources of revenue. This practice makes it hard to manage the activities that generate revenue. Instead, management should show on the budget several categories of sources from which revenues will come. One useful categorization scheme is revenue from existing customers, revenue from new customers, and revenue from various new initiatives. It's important that whatever categories you use do not overlap. You should also include a line for revenue loss, to show the expected drop in revenue from existing customers. Then you must be sure that the budget includes the costs associated with pursuing the initiatives you will undertake to generate the revenue. A budget with this level of detail about the sources of revenue and their costs is what I call a *growth budget.* A growth budget helps leaders understand where revenue growth is coming from so they can make better decisions about how to deploy resources and channel people's energy.

A growth budget will help leaders see the benefits of value creation selling. Initially, the activities associated with a VCS initiative will incur costs and likely produce little in the way of new revenues, but as relationships deepen and you break out of the commodity pricing trap, revenues will rise.

Invariably the question arises about how you will fund a growth initiative like VCS. This is where senior managers must make some make hard decisions. There are two major sources of funding. The most common is productivity improvements, which many companies make routinely every year. The second source is weeding out activities that cause complexity, for example, too many SKUs (stock keeping units) for one product, or too many products in a category (which dilutes the focus), or too many customers that do not meet the minimum criteria for doing business with them.

There is no shirking these decisions; the funding must come from somewhere. CFOs accustomed to cutting costs, not increasing them, might have a particularly hard time creating a growth budget. But those who understand revenue productivity and growth will recognize the limitations of traditional budgeting and drive themselves to find creative solutions to finance growth. Several years ago I was meeting with some people at Colgate when a former student saw me as he passed the open door to our conference room. He stopped to chat for a minute, then said, "Well, I better go, I need to get to work to find some money to fund our growth." He was one of the company's senior finance executives. I realized in that instant that this was a company that was clearly focused on growth as well as productivity.

Drive Value Creation Selling Through Reviews

The necessary changes in psychology, focus, and working relationships get reinforced or undermined in the reviews leaders routinely conduct. Leaders can use budget, operating, and talent reviews to examine the pipeline of sales projects, assess how many are in each phase, and plan future actions. But leaders should also use them to coach the sales teams and assess which sales leaders and team members are grasping VCS and may need to be moved up and who is performing poorly and may need to be moved out.

Typical monthly or quarterly budget and operating reviews are too often backward looking and done in an atmosphere of fear and intimidation. Neither the content nor the atmosphere helps the VCS effort. Instead, budget reviews need to be forward looking and done in the spirit of collaboration that is at the heart of value creation selling. Artful questioning will reveal if the sales teams are hitting barriers and bottlenecks they can't seem to get around. The leader can then use the meeting to guide the team, maybe providing specific advice on how they can gather information and put together a value proposition for a specific customer. Some investigative work ahead of time can help the leader prepare.

Even the types of questions leaders ask can shift people's attention. Asking about revenue-generating techniques or how departments like legal and finance are helping meet customer needs lets everyone know that those things are important.

The tone of these reviews is also important. In the early phases of implementing value creation selling the senior managers need to be alert for signs of discouragement, especially on the part of the sales leader, who is dealing with new concepts and methodologies while leading, probably for the first time, a team of people from other functions and possibly with higher rank. Any evidence that other departments are not collaborating needs to be investigated and remedied immediately.

At the same time, the leaders conducting reviews can discern who seems to have the ability to grasp the basics of business acumen, to gather intelligence on the customer, to analyze the customer's needs, to organize an effective multifunction team without having hierarchical power over it, and, finally, to devise and present to the customer a value proposition. Those insights should inform the decisions made about people in subsequent talent reviews and planning sessions.

In most companies the annual ritual of adjusting salary for the coming year, awarding cash bonuses for the year concluded, and awarding stock or stock options is almost always tied to quantitative measures of performance. Value creation selling is certainly aimed at producing increases in such quantitative measures as revenue and profit margin but other qualitative factors contribute to its success. As a result performance appraisals of sales leaders and their sales team members should incorporate a wider range of variables. These might include the person's business acumen, team-building skills, and ability to lead in a nonhierarchical environment, as well as his ability to build a long-lasting and penetrating relationship with the customer, to imaginatively and creatively craft a value proposition, and to present that proposition persuasively and in terms of the customer's priorities and business needs.

To reinforce VCS, you might want to establish a monthly bell-ringer award for any team that closes a sale in which the value proposition increases the customer's profit margin or profitably increases his revenues. You might consider a bigger reward at the end of the year for all sales leaders who meet these criteria.

Link Compensation

Value creation selling requires a different system for compensation and rewards, so that's another change you must be willing to make. Most compensation and sales incentive programs have been designed around transactional sales. They focus exclusively on quantifiable targets, usually in the form of quotas. VCS programs have quantifiable goals, too, but they are different from transactional goals, and VCS programs also include behavioral goals aimed squarely at getting people to adopt specific behaviors associated with VCS, such as collaboration and reaching out to customers.

Having reorganized its packaging business, Mead-Westvaco began the transition to a VCS strategy in 2006. To support this, the company's human resources team, which performs a vital strategic function at MeadWestvaco, worked with corporate and business unit leadership to review the company's existing sales compensation plans to determine which features might be useful in the new environment and what had to change. It rolled out the new sales incentive plans business unit by business unit, starting with those that were most ready to change and covering most of the packaging businesses in seven months.

"The basic elements of each new plan depend on the business unit," explained Linda Schreiner, senior vice president in charge of human resources. "What's different between the old and new plans is what we're measuring. Now we're rewarding the development of more profitable business sales generated with clear value-driven plans."

Angie Parrish, the MeadWestvaco compensation analyst who headed the effort to create the new plans, said every plan now centers around a profitability measurement. Many still include volume targets for salespeople, but those volume targets come with a "profitability modifier" that drives incentive payments up or down.

Most plans also have a *strategic initiative* component that directly addresses a salesperson's ability to do VCS. "This part of the plan is tied to the planning and performance behaviors we are looking for," Parrish explains. "This includes the quality of account planning, development of contacts with strategic influencers and key decision makers, and presentations that clearly delineate the value of a product or service offering to the customer. Based on these factors, managers evaluate the person's performance at one of three levels: threshold, target, or stretch."

Support functions that were not previously included in sales incentive plans are now part of the reward system, Parrish said, and their compensation is based on the level of their contribution to the sales process. While the "primary" contributors are the salespeople themselves, sales managers, marketing, and technical sales support as well as customer service representatives are all part of the team and eligible for rewards. As the company gains experience with the new plans, people in other functions and roles are likely to be included in the reward system, she said.

Important lessons from MeadWestvaco's experience are choosing the set of measures that reflect what you most want to accomplish, such as upgrading selling skills, improving margins and shifting the product mix, as well as increasing revenues. But don't limit yourself to quantitative measures, and don't forget to reward changes in behavior. Also, include financial and systems expertise early in the planning process so you know for sure that you can measure what you want to measure.

The new compensation plans were introduced early in 2007 and the early results are positive. Happy to see their compensation aligned with what top management is asking them to do, the salespeople themselves have been very receptive to the new compensation plan.

Measuring Success

In VCS, closing a sale is just the beginning. The proof of the pudding is when the customer realizes the benefits you promised. Top management should create some means to measure success for each account, and get the customer's concurrence on it. Teams should be rewarded each time the customer realizes the benefits proposed.

Make no mistake, implementing a value creation selling

strategy is a long-term commitment. The companies that have done it successfully required around three years to become adept at it, and most continue to refine their processes. Success requires constant repetition of the principle that the company will prosper only if its customers prosper—a message that is easier to convey when you begin to score wins.

Senior managers must drive the adoption of value creation selling every inch of the way. They should create a dashboard, or set of metrics, to gauge progress and revisit it at every executive leadership meeting, whether weekly, monthly, or quarterly. Those discussions should address the following questions:

1. Why did we win or lose specific business for which we made a value creation selling pitch?
2. How well has our value creation sales effort penetrated our existing customers?
3. Which existing or potential customers are the next candidates for a value creation sales approach?
4. To which customers are we providing thought leadership?
5. How well is our sales force shaping and customizing a unique value proposition for our customer?
6. How well do we tie our pricing to the attributes our customers value most?
7. How well are our people extracting information about customer needs?
8. Are they relaying that information to the people in our company who can act on it?

Answers to these questions will tell you whether you're progressing. You'll know value creation selling has taken hold when the following things occur:

- The first sales leader is promoted into a nonsales management position.
- Recruiting and training for sales focuses on people who have a fundamental grasp of business acumen and are inclined to be team players and team leaders.
- Recruiting for other functional areas emphasizes collaborative work and imaginative application of specific expertise.
- Customer information flows from the sales force back into product development, marketing, and pricing functions.
- People outside of sales are thinking of ways to meet the customer's needs.
- Your organization is seamlessly connected to the customer at all times.
- The customer calls your company first.
- Customers share information about their future plans because they trust you.
- Customers see you as unique, creating a huge barrier for competitors to break.
- Customers refer you to others because they know you deliver the value you promise.

8

Taking Value Creation Selling
to the Next Level

Sturgis Corporation's progress had attracted the attention not only of headhunters who tried to lure away the company's top salespeople, but also of other companies. Jack Garrett, the CEO, had been both surprised and flattered a few months earlier to get a call from Byron Ault, the chairman of Technologis Corporation, an up-and-coming software developer.

"Jack, I'm hearing great things about how you're transforming Sturgis," Ault said. "We're a little further down the path than you are with value creation selling and I can tell you it works. But that's not why I called. We recently had a director retire from the board and we need a replacement. We stand to gain a lot from your wisdom, judgment, and exemplary leadership. We would be honored to have you join our board. We have a great board and we learn a lot from each other."

Jack had been a little ambivalent about accepting a seat on the board, only because the transformation of Sturgis had been taking almost all his time. He wasn't sure where he would find the time to make the kind of commitment that being a board member of another company required. But Byron Ault sealed the deal over lunch when he discussed how value creation selling was driving his company's growth. Jack figured the time he devoted to the Technologis board would serve Sturgis well.

Byron explained to Jack how Technologis had been on something of a roller-coaster ride. It had prospered during the technology boom of the late 1990s, when its sophisticated software products were in high demand by CIOs with big budgets seeking strategic applications. Then when the crunch came in 2000 and the technology boom went bust, companies facing zero or no growth started reining in costs to regain profitability. Customers that had once been keen on new, unproven technologies started asking for software that would help cut costs.

As Technologis tried to adjust, it had to cut its own costs, which it did mostly by scaling back the sales force. Revenues and profits dwindled. That's when Byron decided to try a value creation selling strategy. The transition was far from easy, he said, but now value creation selling was firmly in place and Technologis was once again thriving.

"At this point in our evolution we're concentrating on making a good thing better," Byron told Jack. "Two years ago I started a benchmarking process, and as part of that I hold an annual event I call customer's summit. It's a cocktails and dinner get-together. I invite some senior people from a dozen or so of our best customers and my senior management team. It includes a one-hour session when I ask the customers to give us some candid feedback on what we can do better and what our competitors are doing better than we are. You're welcome to attend this year's summit to see for yourself how customers think about value creation selling."

Now Jack was on his way to the Regent's Club to sit in on his first customer summit.

There were two dozen people from ten of Technologis's customers and an equal number of Technologis executives hovering over plates of hor d'oeuvres when Jack entered the meeting room. He only had time to introduce himself to a few people before Byron asked them all to take their seats.

Byron set an informal tone right from the start, opening the meeting with a heartfelt thank you to his guests for taking time to come and asking them to introduce themselves to the group one by one. Then he reminded them why they were there: "We want to hear what's on your minds. We hope you'll tell us what we're not doing so well and need to do better, and what we're not doing now and should do to be a long-term partner. Believe me, there's no defensiveness here. We consider your honest thinking a real gift to us. It'll help us get to the next level."

It didn't take long for the CIO of one of Technologis's biggest customers to offer his opinion.

"When I started as CIO five years ago we wanted you to help us achieve savings that we could invest in customer and market development. But cost savings is just a given now. The game has changed and we need to add value to our customers. Your people need to be talking to my people more about how to do that. We need ideas that will improve our business, not just cut our costs. I've seen some real progress in that area over the past three years, but you need to do more. Your people still talk technological mumbo jumbo and my people still do, too, more often than I'd like. We've got to take it to a higher plane where we're both talking about what's happening in our business, and what our industry will look like in two years. We should be looking at what we need to do now to take advantage of the changes that are coming. Basically your people need to learn more about our industry and what's happening in it."

Jack saw that Byron seemed pleased, even as he listened intently to the complaint. "Duly noted," Byron said. "But let me turn the tables just a bit. What if I ask you to sponsor two or three day-long seminars for your top technology people to give our sales team some insights into what is happening and what they think the future holds? Can you devote that much effort to help bring our people up to speed?"

"We might not be able to get all our people together at the same time, but I'll promise you I'll make sure that your team members get time with them, whether in a group or individually," the CIO responded.

Jack noted what Byron had just done: Turned the complaint into an action item that would help penetrate the customer more deeply, perhaps getting meetings with people the sales team hadn't met before. At the same time Technologis would demonstrate its commitment to learn about its customers.

Next to offer an opinion was the chief financial officer at a smaller customer that had been struggling in a very competitive market.

"One thing I like about working with Technologis is that your people aren't afraid to raise issues with us. They don't just salute whatever we say. A lot of your competitors, especially vendors we've dealt with in India, don't like to risk a confrontation and don't bring up issues. That winds up creating problems later when we run into a problem that they could have steered us away from.

"The other thing that's good is that you have cross-functional teams. We love that your teams are coming and working with our teams. The cross-functional work is crucial and we'd like to see more of it."

Jack made a mental note of that remark and the fact that it came from a CFO who was likely influential at his company. Jack had never doubted the wisdom of cross-functional teams and his sales teams seemed to be working well. But he knew that Sturgis's initial foray into value creation selling had tapped his most enthusiastic and capable people. What would happen to collaboration as the number of teams expanded and some included members who weren't as enthusiastic or capable? That was something he'd want to talk to Byron about at some point.

Then the executive vice president of marketing at a retail chain spoke up almost as if to refute the first speaker's remarks about Technologis's grasp of the industry.

"Your people have been the only vendors we deal with who have come up with ideas about how we retailers can make a difference in the marketplace," he said.

"I've been very surprised and pleased at the depth of knowledge Technologis has about retailing. My boss was very pleased when he visited your operations in India, where your people surprised him by constructing a virtual replica of one of our stores."

That comment prompted the CIO of a financial company to speak up.

"Byron, we've been doing business with you now for two years and by and large the experience has been very positive. But I don't share the opinion that your people have deep domain knowledge, at least not as far as the investment banking industry is concerned. I have to say that while your sales team is conversant with technology, they aren't up to speed on the workings of this industry. If I ask them to come with me to meet the investment bankers, who need to approve some purchases, they seem to be out of their league. They need to understand how credit derivatives and swaps work to be able to discuss how the bankers can best use the software."

Jack knew how hard it was to understand derivatives. He observed Byron using the dialogue to seek advice and latching on to a suggestion to hire some people from investment banking to be part of the sales team.

Then another CFO raised his hand. When Byron acknowledged him he said that in the past 10 weeks he had been monitoring the situation in India. The rupee had been revalued by almost 10 percent and another adjustment was expected soon. And Indian labor costs were rising at 20 percent per year.

"I've got to think that those kinds of cost increases

are beginning to squeeze your margins," he told Byron. "Chances are, you're going to want to ask for a price increase. If that's the case, you need to let us know as early as possible. I understand the situation completely, but I need some advance warning so I can make the case in-house that you really need a price increase. A price increase will be very hard for us. What can we do jointly to create a win-win?"

The subject of India prompted a CEO in attendance to bring up his own situation. "We set up some of our own IT operations in India, and it just isn't working out. We can't manage them as effectively from here as we had thought. We'd like to sell those operations to someone with better operating experience in that market. If you're interested, Byron, call me."

The meeting went on for the full two hours, a mix of compliments, complaints, suggestions, and questions. Byron handled the dialogue with aplomb, promising to take the complaints to heart and acknowledging the compliments with modest appreciation. Throughout it all Jack had been unobtrusively taking notes, and during dinner he quizzed his dining partners on how their relationships with Technologis had developed.

It occurred to Jack that it wasn't enough to want to share information; you had to be proactive about ensuring that the sharing happened. He'd have to brief his senior management on that point. If we let customers know we're thinking about making a change in something, he thought, they might be able to steer us away from making a bad decision.

The meeting was winding toward a close, but two

customers still had their hands up. Byron pointed to the woman first.

"I don't have a complaint, Byron, so don't look so concerned," she laughed. "I just want to say that one of the things I appreciate most about dealing with your sales team is that they're always prepared when they come to a meeting. They get right to the point and they don't waste our time. They aren't afraid to tell us when they think we're taking the wrong direction and they have good reasons for arguing the point." She also noted that it was easy for her or one of her direct reports to reach the right person in Technologis. "Your people are empowered to make decisions and we don't have to go through multiple layers of bureaucracy to get something fixed."

Finally, Technologis's CFO and general counsel were the subject of effusive praise.

"As you know, we have some pretty complicated contracts for sourcing," said the senior legal officer for a manufacturer of switching equipment. "I can't say enough good things about your CFO and general counsel. With other vendors the contracts go through five thousand layers and it takes weeks to get them signed. With you it takes a matter of days and they go out of their way to be flexible and accommodate our needs. They negotiate hard, but they're fair and I think we both come away with what we need."

Later as Jack was driving home from the summit he realized two things. First, Sturgis had a lot more work to do to on value creation selling. He knew now that the time he devoted to his position as a director of Technologis would be invaluable in helping guide Sturgis's transition. Second, he knew now, more than ever, that his decision to take Sturgis into value creation selling was the right one. Then he began to think about how soon he could hold his own customer summit. He could barely wait. He would hold them twice a year and invite his board.

Jack gripped the steering wheel with one hand and held a small voice recorder in the other, dictating notes to himself about what he had learned that day.

"I've got to make sure we have the necessary industry knowledge about each of our customers. If we don't, we'll either have to bring our teams up to speed or hire the expertise from outside.

"Customers really value meeting commitments and showing flexibility. I need to make sure we're pushing decision making far enough down into the organization so that customers can get things fixed fast.

"Customers want to know in advance when changes are coming. We've got to make sure we all understand that, because it's part of building trust. It's easy to forget to let them know what we're planning to do.

"I need to reemphasize to the sales teams that they should feel free to raise issues with the customers early in the process. Better that than to let them become bigger problems later.

"Cross-functional teams are the way to go, but I've got to be sure that as we create more teams we have the kind of enthusiastic and capable people who will make them work.

"The customer summit is a great idea, especially bringing in the board. We need to set one up as soon as possible. Getting that kind of feedback is the next step in value creation selling."

Transforming a sales force from transactional selling to one that creates value for the customer is a long journey. It requires a huge change in the way a company thinks and operates. Every part of the company has to put the customer first. The Sturgis Corporation is a fictional name, but the story is real and shows the level of energy and the relentless commitment that top management has to make for value creation selling to take hold.

As you set off on your journey, you'll no doubt encounter obstacles along the way. Senior management will be challenged to find the right compensation system to properly reward such sales support functions as legal, finance, product development, and human resources. Sales leaders will have to find ways to develop relationships with people other than the gatekeepers in the customer's shop. Your company will have to pinpoint the customers who are willing to develop a trusting relationship and find alternative ways to serve other customers. You will have to create and sustain an environment that encourages creativity and imagination in formulating value propositions. All the while, senior managers must think hard and carefully about the future of their own company, what markets it will serve and what products or services it will develop. Committed leaders will find answers to the problems and ways around the obstacles.

The good news is that the journey is difficult and requires persistence and tenacity. That's good news because it means not everyone can or will make that journey, and those who do will be amply rewarded. I have watched companies like Unifi, MeadWestvaco, and Thomson Financial find prosperity through value creation selling. Having left the gate early, they have an edge.

Virtually every company will have among its customers some who are progressive and fully understand the value of collaborating with their suppliers to the mutual benefit of both. Start there, and don't turn back. A company that successfully implements value creation selling will have a new, potent source of management talent, a critical competitive advantage in a world short of leadership. Above all, value creation selling will spur your company to come up with new ideas and innovations that will continually differentiate it in the highly competitive business environment of the twenty-first century. It is the pathway to a prosperous future.

The End of the Story

October was a good month for Sturgis. Third quarter results showed a decidedly upward turn in both revenue and profit, and the company was ratcheting up projections based on deepening relationships with several large customers, including a few Sturgis had nearly lost. Just days after the earnings release, Susan stopped by to tell Jack that one of the sales teams had signed a four-year contract with Tri-Net, the biggest ever. The news prompted Jack to write congratulatory notes to all the team members, but he had a special message for Charlie Baldwin, the team leader.

Dear Charlie:

Congratulations on your success with Tri-Net. You have done a terrific job of drawing the best out of the people at Sturgis and showing Tri-Net how we can help them pursue a whole new market segment to achieve their goal of revenue growth.

This contract is important to us not just because of its dollar value (which is considerable) but also because of what it represents: how we will create a better future for our customers and ourselves. It shows the value of building relationships at many levels in the customer shop and the importance of breaking down silos here at Sturgis. If we do that consistently, we will find ways to tap the tremendous capabilities of our people to create unique offerings that command the premium pricing we deserve.

It is gratifying to see how much you've grown in the past year and a half. You have become a pace-setter for the entire value creation selling effort. We are lucky to have you.

I hope you take a well deserved vacation.

Best regards,
Jack

Charlie read the note while Michelle was making reservations for a hotel in Paris. Value creation selling was working. The company's new compensation plan was working. Work was fun again. Life was good.

Appendix: How Far Are You with Value Creation Selling?

This instrument can help you diagnose the state of value creation selling in your company. Done four times a year (at least until VCS is well under way), it will give you a basis for comparing progress from one period to another. You can also use it to assess yourself against the competition.

Answer the following questions using a scale of 1 to 10, from "definitely not" to "definitely yes."

1. Are we getting premium pricing or preventing commoditization in the pricing of our offerings?

2. Has sales management mastered the details and framework of VCS:

   a. at the executive level?
   b. at the regional level?
   c. at the district level?

3. Is our sales force focused on the right segment and set of customers for VCS?

4. According to customer feedback, are our value propositions of high quality and appropriate:

   a. in terms of the customer's priorities?
   b. in terms of the physical definition?
   c. in terms of financial and quantifiable benefits for customers, particularly revenue growth?
   d. in terms of intangible benefits like brand equity?

5. Is the sales force effective in creating and presenting a value account plan (VAP)?

6. Are sales leaders effective in pulling together internal resources to create and pitch the value proposition?

7. Is the win ratio high?

8. Are value creation activities linked to:

   a. budgeting?
   b. operating reviews?
   c. diagnosis of lost sales?
   d. the reward system?
   e. executive committee meetings?

9. Do support functions and activities practice value creation selling and contribute to the VAP?

10. Is our value creation selling effort effective in the eyes of our customers?

11. Are our people building social networks at multiple levels and in multiple areas of the customer?

12. Do our sales leaders do well in dissecting the decision-making process and identifying the decision makers in the customer's organization?

13. Is there a high level of trust between us and the customer?

14. Do customers seek our advice and counsel?

15. Is the pipeline of sales leaders becoming a source of talent for leadership positions beyond sales?

Acknowledgments

This book would not have been possible without the generosity of some very accomplished business leaders who shared their precious time and learning with me for the sake of helping others improve. I am deeply grateful for the tremendous contribution the following individuals have made to the book: Tim Ahern, Jim Buzzard, Ken Claflin, Mark Cross, Lou Eccleston, Bob Feezer, Dick Harrington, Ben Holder, Clayton LiaBraaten, John Luke, Gary Mulloy, Ralph Olson, Brian Parke, Angie Parrish, Jay Robertson, Linda Schreiner, Dennis Simon, Jim Smith, and Bob Whitman.

I am fortunate to have had the editorial talents of Doug Sease and Geri Willigan to make the ideas and tools presented here clear and accessible. A skillful writer and reporter, Doug worked diligently to transform copious notes and discussions into eminently readable text. Geri, working closely with me as she has for more than a decade, helped sharpen and structure the ideas and ensured that the final product would be both engaging and educational. Charlie Burck, an editorial ace, and John Joyce, my long-time friend, made very helpful contributions as well.

I owe a great deal of appreciation to my editors, Adrian Zackheim and Jeffrey Krames, who encouraged me to pursue this project and helped shape the content of the book, and to Courtney Young for her editorial and production assistance.

Finally, a heartfelt thank you to Cynthia Burr, Karen Baker, and Carol Davis, the exceptionally talented and dedicated people in my Dallas office, who provided many forms of administrative support throughout the project.

Index

About the Author

Ram Charan is a world-renowned adviser to business leaders and corporate boards, a best-selling author, and an award-winning teacher. He is known for his keen insights into business problems and his real-world practicality in solving them.

Jack Welch has said he is "a huge admirer" of Ram's and notes that Ram has a rare ability "to distill meaningful from meaningless" and is unusually adept at helping companies adopt best practices. He said Ram helped "stimulate his thinking" and that he "loved batting ideas around with Ram."

Fortune magazine said Ram is a "wise man," one of the "most influential consultants alive," and a leading expert in corporate governance.

Business Week put him in the top five teachers in the United States for in-house executive development programs.

The Economist referred to Ram as a veteran of CEO succession planning.

For nearly four decades, Ram has advised some of the world's most successful business leaders on far-ranging issues, from corporate governance and CEO selection to changing corporate culture and pursuing organic growth. He has worked behind the scenes at companies such as General Electric, Verizon, DuPont, and Colgate.

Ram's solutions are highly pragmatic, largely because of his field research approach: observing real-life actions and extracting what works.

Ram is also a prolific writer, having authored or coauthored fourteen books, including *Know-How* and *What the CEO Wants You to Know. Execution,* written with former Honeywell CEO Larry Bossidy, was on the *New York Times* best-seller list for nearly three years and has two million copies in print. Ram has contributed front cover articles to *Fortune, Harvard Business Review,* and many other publications.

Ram's interactive style and practicality have made him a favorite among executive educators. He has taught for thirty consecutive years at GE's John F. Welch learning center in Crotonville, New York, and has won best teacher awards at Wharton and Northwestern.

Ram's business career started when he was just a teenager working in the family shoe shop in India. He went on to earn an engineering degree and then master's of business administration and doctorate degrees from Harvard Business School. He graduated from Harvard with high distinction and was a Baker Scholar.

Ram is a director of Austin Industries, Tyco Electronics, and Emaar Manufacturing in India. He was elected a Distinguished Fellow of the National Academy of Human Resources in 2005. He is based in Dallas, Texas.